Sixty-Six Days, Sixty-Six Books

A Brief Message From Each Book of the Bible

by

Lloyd D. Grimm, Jr.

Schmul Publishing Company
Nicholasville, Kentucky

Published by Schmul Publishing Co.
PO Box 776
Nicholasville, KY USA

Printed in the United States of America

ISBN 10: 0-88019-471-5
ISBN 13: 978-0-88019-471-6

Visit us on the Internet at www.wesleyanbooks.com, or order direct from the publisher by calling 800-772-6657, or by writing to the above address.

Contents

A Brief Message From Each Book of the Bible

***God, who at sundry times and in divers manners spake in times past unto the fathers by the prophets, hath in these last days spoken unto us by His Son* (Hebrews 1:12).**

It was approximately seventy years ago that God for Christ's sake saved my soul. As a young boy I experienced deep conviction, and as a result I sought God with no human help as I prayed. However, I had told my mother of my deep feelings and she instructed me how to pray. My prayer was simple but peace came to my soul. Later at the age of thirteen I felt the need for a deeper work of grace. Again my mother told me what to do in order to be sanctified wholly. Again my prayer was simple but effective. I don't think I had emotion at the time, but it was a stabilizing experience.

I felt the call to the ministry at about nineteen or twenty years of age. I preached my first message at the age of twenty-one and took my first pastorate at the age of twenty-two. At this writing I am seventy-seven and have been active in the pastorate and other ministries nearly all the intervening time since I took my first church in 1945.

I have made it a practice for many years to read my Bible through each year. As a result there are some passages that speak forcefully to my own heart. God has put it in my heart at this late period of my life to write a message from each of the sixty-six books of the Bible.

As the reader will notice this is not written in a scholarly fashion, but perhaps more as a testimony to God's goodness and faithfulness and the lessons He has taught me through these many years. "*Thy word is a lamp unto my feet, and a light unto my path*" (Psalm 119:105). "*The Lord bless thee, and keep thee: The Lord make his face shine upon thee, and be gracious unto thee: The Lord lift up his countenance upon thee, and give thee peace*" (Numbers 6:24-26).

—Lloyd D. Grimm Jr.
Retired Elder in
The Church of the Nazarene

Christlike Forgiveness

Background Scripture: Genesis 37, 39-50

***And when Joseph's brethren saw that their father was dead, they said, Joseph will peradventure hate us, and will certainly requite us all the evil which we did unto him. And they sent a messenger unto Joseph, saying, Thy father did command before he died, saying, So shall ye say unto Joseph, Forgive, I pray thee now, the trespass of thy brethren, and their sin; for they did unto thee evil and now, we pray thee, forgive the trespass of the servants of the God of thy father. And Joseph wept when they spake unto him. And his brethren also went and fell down before his face; and they said, Behold, we be thy servants. And Joseph said unto them, Fear not, for am I in the place of God? But as for you, ye thought evil against me; but God meant it unto good, to bring to pass, as it is this day, to save much people alive. Now therefore fear ye not: I will nourish you, and your little ones. And he comforted them, and spake kindly into them* (Genesis 50:15-21).**

Booker T. Washington was born into slavery, but he arose above his environment, allowing no amount of prejudice and hatred to detour him from his purpose in life, and like Abel of old, "*...he being dead yet speaketh*" (Hebrews 11:4b). Many years ago a young Hebrew servant had evidently arrived at the same conclusion, for no matter how harshly he was treated, Joseph displayed no evidence of malice and retaliation, but only love and genuine forgiveness.

As his brothers sold him to a company of Ishmaelites they noted the anguish of his soul as they testified later in recounting their evil deed. Although his own flesh and blood brothers tortured him, selling him as a slave, Potiphar's wife falsely accused him, and his fellow prisoner forgot him in his crisis, yet Joseph was consistent in displaying a Christlike attitude in an age even before the law was given. In a pre-Pentecostal dispensation his life exemplified holiness in action. Joseph was determined to follow God regardless of the cost in personal sacrifice.

This young man had learned by hard and difficult experiences that God has a master plan that no man can thwart. When Joseph's brethren prostrated themselves before him and offered to become his servants, *"Joseph said unto them, Fear not: for am I in the place of God? But as ye thought evil against me; but God meant it unto good, to pass, as it is this day, to save much people alive"* (Genesis 50:19-20). Joseph viewed providential crises from God's perspective. He was living so close to his Creator that he was enabled to see God as salvaging good from this difficult situation that took place in Israel's household.

We see examples in our day how God has turned the wrath of men from their evil designs into that which will bring salvation and glorify God. Some of us remember the dark days and awful suffering of World War II when it looked like even civilization was threatened. Yet, we see how God's kingdom was extended during those difficult and troublesome times. The denomination of which I am a member planted a church in Italy because one of our servicemen who was stationed in that country had a vision for the lost of that nation. The Psalmist wrote that, *"Surely the wrath of man shall praise Thee"* (Psalm 76:10a). In the above incidences we see this truth literally fulfilled.

Let us follow Joseph's example in looking at the events in our lives, which we do not understand from God's perspective, and believe His word "that all things work together for good to them, *that love God, to them that are the called according to His purpose"* (Romans 8:28). Because of Joseph's love and Christlike forgiveness, God was enabled to save His people from destruction and through the tribe of Judah give us His only Begotten Son to save the world.

Sing Unto The Lord
(Psalm 30:4a)

I do not ask to choose my path.
Lord, lead me in Thy way;
Inspire each tho't and prompt each word,
And make me a blessing today.[1]

Verse to Memorize: *And be ye kind one to another, tenderhearted, forgiving one another, even as God for Christ's sake hath forgiven you* (Ephesians 4:32).

No Other Way

Background Scripture: Exodus 11-12

***For I will pass through the land of Egypt this night, and will smite all the firstborn in the land of Egypt, both man and beast; and against all the gods of Egypt I will execute judgment: I am the Lord. And the blood shall be to you for a token upon the houses where ye are: and when I see the blood, I will pass over you, and the plague shall not destroy you, when I smite the land of Egypt* (Exodus 12:12-13).**

Man's basic problem is sin. The consequences of sin is death in its totality: physical, spiritual, and eternal. In order to abolish the effects of sin, the basic problem must be dealt with. Without Christ man is in a dilemma. John Bunyan, in his allegory, pictures Christian standing in the field, his face from his own home, clad in rags with a burden on his back and a Book in his hands. He looked this way and that way as if he would run, yet did not, for he knew not which way to flee. He wept bitterly. An evangelist approached him and said, "Wherefore dost thou cry?"

"Sir," said he, "I perceive by this Book in my hand that I am condemned to die, and after that to come into judgment; and I find that I am not willing to do the first, nor able to do the second, and the thought of these things make me cry."[1]

Alas, this is the condition of everyone who is enlightened, but not justified. Is there a satisfactory answer to this predicament? I am very sincere when I say there is only one answer, and that is the blood of Jesus Christ. As the death angel passed over Egypt that awful night there was only one exception in order for the firstborn to live: "W*hen I see the blood, I will pass over you...*" (Exodus 12:13).

All of these animal sacrifices would have no significance whatsoever, except as they pointed to the true sacrifice, "*the Lamb of God, which taketh away the sin of the world*" (John 1:29b). The inspired writer of Hebrews points out that the law of sacrifices was a shadow of good things to come. That good has come in the person of Jesus Christ. Nathaniel asked the question, "*Can any good thing come out of Nazareth? Philip saith unto him, Come and see" (John* 1:46). There is no use of arguing and debating, but heed the advice of the anointed Psalmist, *"O taste and see that the Lord is good: blessed is the man that trusteth in Him"* (Psalm 34:8).

Why not pray the prayer of the publican who called on God and said, "*God be merciful to me a sinner?"* (Luke 18:13b) Jesus tells us "*this man went down to his house justified..."* (Luke 18:1). This is the way and the only way to find a satisfactory answer to life's deepest problems. Jesus says, "*Verily, verily, I say unto you, He that heareth my word, and believeth on Him that sent me, hath everlasting life, and shall not come into condemnation, but is passed from death unto life"* (John 5:24).

Sing unto the Lord (Psalm 30:4a)

What can wash away my sin?
Nothing but the blood of Jesus.
What can make me whole again?
Nothing but the blood of Jesus.[2]

Verses to Memorize: *Forasmuch then as the children are partakers of flesh and blood, He also Himself took part of the same; that through death He might destroy him that had the power of death, that is the devil; And deliver them who through fear of death were all their lifetime subject to bondage* (Hebrew 2:14-15).

A Genuine Cure for Sin

Background Scripture: Leviticus 5:7-10

For if the blood of bulls and of goats, and the ashes of an heifer sprinkling the unclean, sanctifieth to the purifying of the flesh: How much more shall the blood of Christ, who through the eternal Spirit offered himself without spot to God, Purge your conscience from dead works to serve the living God? (Hebrews 9:13-14)

The rivers of blood that flowed from the veins of the multitude of sacrificed animals would be of no avail for sin except as the Israelites trusted and believed in their Messiah yet to come, "*the Lamb of God, which taketh away the sin of the world*" (John 1:29b). In order to understand the Book of Leviticus in the Old Testament we must look to the Book of Hebrews in the New Testament. This inspired New Testament Epistle is a commentary on the Book of Leviticus. Here we see the contrast of the old letter of the law and the new and living way Christ opened to every believer. We read, "*Having therefore, brethren, boldness to enter into the holiest by the blood of Jesus, by a new and living way, which He hath consecrated for us, through the veil, that is to say, His flesh*" (Hebrews 10:19-20).

As we read and study the vicarious sacrifice of Christ and all the preparation God made in the law for the coming of the Savior which St. Paul refers to as, "*our schoolmaster to bring us unto Christ, that we might be justified by faith*" (Galatians 3:24b), we readily see the hideousness of sin.

If sin is nothing more than weakness, or a mal-adjustment in our nature that can be corrected by education and improving our living conditions, then we have no need to be overly concerned, but if it is a deadly virus eating away at the very core of our being, then we need to flee from the wrath to come and take refuge in the redemption God has provided by giving His only Begotten Son for the life of the world.

I fear we pass by the events of the cross too lightly and do not comprehend the cost involved to save us from sin and its consequences. We can only get a portrait of what sin actually is as we see the suffering our blessed Lord and Savior Jesus Christ endured in Gethsemane and on the cross. We see not only the physical suffering, but the mental and spiritual torment as He died and experienced the very pangs of hell as for a brief time He suffered what is the very essence of hell in being separated from His Father as Jesus cried out, *"...My God, my God, why hast Thou forsaken me?"* (Matthew 27:46b) Why? Why? The only answer is that God loves us and desires to save us from living and dying in sin. May we all bow in humble adoration, and from our hearts say with St. Paul, "*Thanks be unto God for his unspeakable gift*" (II Corinthians 9-15).

Sing unto the Lord
(Psalm 30:4a)

There is a fountain filled with blood
Drawn from Immanuel's veins;
and sinners plunged beneath that flood,
Lose all their guilty stains.[1]

Verse to Memorize: *Come now, and let us reason together, saith the Lord: though your sins be as scarlet, they shall be as white as snow; though they be red like crimson, they shall be as wool* (Isaiah 1:18).

A Worthy Goal

Background Scripture: Numbers 22-24

***...Let me die the death of the righteous, and let my last end be like his!* (Numbers 23:10b)**

In this scripture we find perhaps the most controversial prophet in all the Word of God. Balaam was trying to hold on to two worlds and in the process it appears he may have lost both of them. In chapter 24 verses 17-19 God through Balaam gave us one of the clearest prophecies concerning the coming Messiah, our Lord Jesus Christ, yet over and over again Balaam tries to see how close he can come to the world of sin, and still retain the approval of God.

Balak asked Balaam to curse God's people. The prophet in chapter 22:8 told the messengers to... "*Lodge here this night, and I will bring you word again, as the Lord shall speak unto me....*" There are some things we already know the course to take and need not pray about. Balaam knew it was not God's will to curse His people Israel. He should have said an emphatic no and settled the issue. Instead Balaam kept asking for the will of God many times when God had clearly shown him the course he should take. It is possible for us to continue to beg God for our own way until God grants our request to our souls detriment. This happened in the history of Israel. We read, "*And He gave them their request; but sent leanness into their soul*" (Psalm 106:15). Jesus made it clear that "*no man can serve two masters: for either he will hate the one, and love the other; or else he will hold to the one, and despise the other. Ye cannot serve God and mammon*" (Matthew 6:24).

Balaam did not literally curse Israel, but he did worse. He suggested that if the enemy could persuade Israel to practice idolatry and the worship practiced in Baal-peor they would bring the wrath of God upon them. Israel's enemies followed this evil suggestion, but what happened to the prophet Balaam. Did he reach his goal to die the death of the righteous? No, the children of Israel slew Balaam. We read "...*Balaam also the son of Beor they slew with the sword*" (Numbers 31:8b).

If we plan on dying the death of the righteous then we had better know Christ and live the life of the righteous.

In Psalm 116: 15 we read, "*Precious in the sight of the Lord is the death of His saints*." In the course of a long ministry I knew of many who died triumphantly in the Lord. I will give an account of just one among the many. When I was a young man preparing for the ministry, I met a wonderful outstanding young man who loved God with all his heart. He had attended college a few years before I arrived, and befriended me and helped me in those early days. Edmund Day took suddenly sick and had surgery, but his blood vessel collapsed and he went to be with the Lord. Here was a fine young man equipped for the ministry, serving God and seemingly had his life before him. Did he "die the death of the righteous?" Yes, for on his death bed he quoted the words of St. Paul in Philippians 1:21, "*For to me to live is Christ, and to die is gain*."

Yes, God has made provision through Jesus Christ for all to die the death of the righteous, but the decision rests with each individual.

Sing unto the Lord
(Psalm 30:4a)

Some day the silver cord will break,
And I no more as now shall sing,
But, oh, the joy when I shall wake
Within the palace of the King![1]

Verses to Memorize: *And they stoned Stephen, calling upon God and saying, Lord Jesus receive my spirit. And he kneeled down, and cried with a loud voice, Lord lay not this sin to their charge. And when he had said this, he fell asleep* (Acts 7:59-60).

The Danger of Complacency

***As an eagle stirreth up her nest, fluttereth over her young, spreadeth abroad her wings, taketh them, beareth them on her wings: So the Lord alone did lead him, and there was no strange god with him* (Deuteronomy 32:11-12).**

General William Booth of the Salvation Army observed that fire has a tendency to go out, and applied this truth to show the need of rekindling or adding fresh fuel to our spiritual experience. St. Paul writes to faithful young Timothy, "*Wherefore I put thee in remembrance that thou stir up the gift of God, which is in thee by the putting on of my hands*" (II Timothy 1-6).

In my younger days I remember of banking the furnace so as to keep it burning low but alive with fire until morning. In the morning it was necessary to shake it, poke the low burning coal, and remove the clinkers, the residue that was left as the coal burned itself out. After this, fresh coal was added and soon the flames were leaping and the house was again warm.

The Psalmist said, "*I shall be anointed with fresh oil*" (Psalm 92:10b). Here we see the necessity of keeping our spiritual experience fresh and vital. Dr. J.B. Chapman, late General Superintendent of the Church of the Nazarene, said that a wise General never defends too long a line. Personally it has been nearly seventy years since God for Christ's sake saved my soul, but I am not content to rest alone on that wonderful experience, but I must hear from God today, and I do! Much has happened since my early conversion and the line is long, so I do not attempt to defend such a long line, but I rest on the fact that the blood of Jesus Christ cleanses me at this moment.

In one scripture we see the metaphor God uses of the faithful parent eagle to convey the faithfulness of God in teaching and leading His people so as to develop the spiritual stamina we need in order to serve Him in this present sinful world and have the preparation necessary to hear the "*...Well done, thou good and faithful servant*" (Matthew 25:21) as we change our residence to a permanent and better world.

In order to do this God allows some things to enter our lives that are difficult and hard to understand, and stirs up our comfortable nest in order that we may grow strong spiritually. Satan would attempt to sift and destroy us during these times, but God uses these experiences for our good to strengthen us even as the eagle stirs up her nest but stays close by as she teaches her young to fly. If they should begin to falter she bears them on her wings until they learn to fly. Even so God is ever near us and ready to succor us if we stumble in the process.

Holiness or entire sanctification is both instantaneous and progressive. When one experiences the fiery baptism of the Holy Spirit purifying the heart by faith as we read in Acts 15:9, one will never be more pure than at this moment, but there are many imperfections which are not carnal but human. God permits events to enter our lives that will cause us to grow in our experience as we love and serve Him. After the children of Israel gained possession of Canaan there were still some pockets of resistance left. What do we do with such? We use them. We do as Israel did with the inhabitants of Gibeon who deceived God's people. We read in Joshua 9:21, "*...Let them live, but let them be hewers of wood and drawers of water unto all the congregation.*" We are not speaking of sin remaining but of weakness, though not sinful, yet needs correction.

How then can we use these so-called handicaps or weaknesses? We can help others by testifying how God helped us to overcome and grow in holiness. Paul writes to the Corinthians, "*Who comforteth us in all our tribulation, that we may be able to comfort them which are in any trouble, by the comfort wherewith we ourselves are comforted of God* (II Corinthians 1:4).

God will never permit us to become complacent or self-satisfied, but will keep us dependent on Him by stirring up our comfortable nest as an eagle in order that we may grow in the grace and knowledge of our Lord Jesus Christ.

Sing unto the Lord
(Psalm 30:4a)

Revive us again;
Fill each heart with thy love;
May each soul be rekindled
With fire from above.[1]

Verse to Memorize: *Wilt Thou not revive us again: that Thy people may rejoice in Thee*? (Psalm 85:6)

Take Courage

Background Scripture: Joshua 1:1-9

***There shall not any man be able to stand before thee all the days of thy life: as I was with Moses, so I will be with thee: I will not fail thee. Be strong and of a good courage* (Joshua 1:5-6a).**

The morale of an army has much to do as to whether they are victorious or suffer defeat at the hands of the enemy. This fact is so evident that God commanded Israel to discharge all the fearful and fainthearted from service as the army left to battle the foe. *"And the officers shall speak further unto the people, and they shall say, What man is there that is fearful and fainthearted? let him go and return unto his house, lest his brethren's heart faint as well as his heart" (Deuteronomy 20:8).* Fear and doubt are contagious; and have a strong negative influence for evil, even as faith and trust have a powerful positive influence for good. One of our pastors who had previously been in the military service of our country, and had held some rank in that position, told how they as officers were trained not to show fear as leaders. Fear has a paralyzing effect.

Not only is this true with nations as they war, but it is also true in the spiritual warfare we are engaged in against Satan and the forces of evil. Paul writes, "*Put on the whole armour of God, that ye may be able to stand against the wiles of the devil*" (Ephesians 6:11). Then in verse 16 we read, "*Above all taking the shield of faith, wherewith ye shall be able to quench all the fiery darts of the wicked.*" An optimistic outlook has a powerful influence in overcoming the satanic forces of evil. In Psalm 27:13-14 David said, *"I had fainted, unless I had believed to see the goodness of the Lord in the land of the living. Wait on the Lord: be of good courage and He shall strengthen thine heart: wait, I say, on the Lord."*

God has not promised to shield us from warfare, but He has promised to be with us. Dwight D. Eisenhower in his book, *Crusade in Europe*, tells how one night soon after the initial landing in France a heavy battle was taking place in one sector and, as his custom was, he set out in the twilight to get a firsthand look at it. Along the way the jeep in which he was riding bogged down and he joined a company of infantrymen marching to the front. Soon he found himself walking alongside a big private, and fell into conversation with him. The private's teeth chattered as he talked, not having noticed who was beside him, for from up ahead there came the steady roar of the conflict into which he was entering, perhaps for the first time.

Noting the tremor in the big fellow's voice, the general said, "Are you a bit scared, fellow?"

Just then the private turned to his questioner and for the first time saw by whose side he was walking. He straightened up, the tremor went out of his voice, and he said, "I was, Sir. But I ain't anymore."[1]

We as Christians have nothing to fear so long as we stay close to Christ. "*...If God be for us, who can be against us?*" (Romans 8:31b) Also, we read, "*...for He hath said, I will never leave thee, nor forsake thee*" (Hebrews 13-5b)

Sing unto the Lord
(Psalm 30:4a)

Stand up, stand up for Jesus. The trumpet call obey;
Forth to the mighty conflict, In this His glorious day.
"Ye that are men now serve Him," Against unnumbered foes:
Let courage rise with danger, And strength to strength oppose.[2]

Verse to Memorize: *Have not I commanded thee? Be strong and of a good courage; be not afraid, neither be thou dismayed: for the Lord thy God is with thee whithersoever thou goest* (Joshua 1-9).

A Solo Flight

***In those days there was no king in Israel: every man did that which was right in his own eyes* (Judges 21-25).**

We are headed for difficult and troublesome times when every man is a law unto himself. The refrain "*there was no king in Israel*" is mentioned at least three other times in the Book of Judges; Chapter 17:6, 18:1a, 19:1. As a result we read of hideous accounts of what took place during the period of the judges.

God has put His stamp of approval upon the collective conscience of the church guided by the Holy Spirit. In the early church when a dispute arose between the Jewish and Gentile Christians concerning circumcision and keeping the Law of Moses, we find "*The apostles and elders came together for to consider of this matter*" (Acts 15:6). Then we read, "*For it seemed good to the Holy Ghost, and us, to lay upon you no greater burden than these necessary things*" (Acts 15:28). So collectively the church guided by the Holy Spirit arrived at a satisfactory decision that God continues to honor.

Yet to this day we find those who are making decisions as they did during the times of the judges when men did what seemed right in their own eyes. In one of my pastorates, I called on a man who no longer attended the public worship of God. I invited him to come to our church, but he said he had been to various churches and they had trouble everywhere he went, so he decided to serve God at home. I hasten to say he was surely confused in his theology. On the stormy ocean of life, I would rather stay aboard the big ship than jump overboard and paddle my own little canoe.

We must be careful when we say the Lord told me to take a certain course of action. It should be as thoroughly tested as drugs are before being dispensed. In his book, entitled *Impressions*, Martin Wells Knapp gives four questions we should ask in deciding if an impression is from God. They are: 1. Is it scriptural?, 2. Is it right?, 3. Is it reasonable?, and 4. Is it providential?

Sing unto the Lord
(Psalm 30:4a)

Guide me, O Thou great Jehovah, Pilgrim thru this barren land.
I am weak, but Thou art mighty. Hold me with Thy pow'rful hand.
Bread of heaven, Feed me till I want no more.
Bread of heaven, Feed me till I want no more.[1]

Verse to Memorize: *Wherefore be ye not unwise, but understanding what the will of the Lord is* (Ephesians 5:17).

Ruth

A Living Epistle

Background Scripture: Ruth 1-4

And Boaz answered and said unto her, It hath fully been shewed me, all that thou hast done unto thy mother-in-law since the death of thine husband: and how thou hast left thy father and thy mother, and the land of thy nativity, and art come unto a people which thou knewest not heretofore **(Ruth 2:11).**

The influence of a Godly life extends itself through the remainder of all eternity, and like Abel, "*he being dead yet speaketh*" (Hebrews 11:4a). This life hidden in Christ will be recognized by all though some who are bound by the chains of sin may not acknowledge it. As the world beholds such Christlike living they will be forced to conclude as in the case of Peter and John, "*that they had been with Jesus*" (Acts 4:13b).

Counterfeiting the genuine Spirit filled Christian is impossible. If attempted, those who are spiritually minded will detect it immediately. Years ago as a young person I was taught by my Sunday School teacher the distinction between character and reputation. The teacher said character is what you are, but reputation is what people think you are. Ruth was a young woman of genuine character, but she also had a good reputation as Boaz told Ruth how her Godly living had "fully been shown" him.

Most people are not reading the Bible, but men and women are carefully observing the Christian's daily walk. In one of his pastorates, the minister had a little girl attending who thought her pastor was Jesus. What would it do to that child's faith if she had seen in his life that which did not correspond to what he was teaching?

We read, "*Favour is deceitful, and beauty is vain: but a woman that feareth the Lord, she shall be praised*" (Proverbs 31:30). Ruth was such a woman although from the country of Moab, and a foreigner to Israel. Yet, God used her for she yielded her life to Israel's true and living God, and through her seed according to the flesh Jesus Christ was born and gave His life for our sins.

May we all so love and serve God that the world looking on may see the beauty of Jesus in our daily walk, and be drawn to Him.

Sing unto the Lord (Psalm 30:4a)

Let the beauty of Jesus be seen in me
All His wonderful passion and purity!
O Thou Spirit divine, all my nature refine
Till the beauty of Jesus be seen in me.[1]

Verse to Memorize: *Ye are the light of the world. A city that is set on an hill cannot be hid* (Matthew 5:14).

Retaining Our Crown

Background Scripture: I Samuel 9-16

And the Spirit of the Lord will come upon thee, and thou shalt prophesy with them, and shalt be turned into another man **(I Samuel 10:6).**

And the Spirit of God came upon him… **(I Samuel 16:10).**

But the Spirit of the Lord departed from Saul, and an evil spirit from the Lord troubled him **(I Samuel 16:14).**

…God is departed from me, and answereth me no more… **(I Samuel 28:15).**

These Scriptures refer to King Saul, the first king of Israel. According to God's word he was a choice young man serving God with all humility. What could have happened that caused such a drastic change in the life of this fine young man? We read, "*And the Spirit of God came upon him,*" then later it is recorded, "*But the Spirit of the Lord departed from Saul.*" According to Saul's own confession God had departed from him and did not answer him anymore. God is not quick to depart; in fact, it is the individual that leaves God. In Saul's case it is the same as with all who backslide and get away from God or try to live independently of God. In offering the sacrifice, which did not pertain to the king, Saul in essence was saying I no longer need Divine guidance in my life, or I am in control of my life and not God. Pride caused the downfall of Lucifer and all since.

What is the antidote or what can we as God's people do in order that we may retain our crown promised to those who endure unto the end? After relating the apostasy of men and angels, Jude gives us a recipe for saving ourselves from the fate of those apostates he mentions in his epistle. "*But ye, beloved building up yourselves on your most holy faith, praying in the Holy Ghost, keep yourselves in the love of God, looking for the mercy of our Lord Jesus Christ unto eternal life*" (Verses 20-21).

During the times of bereavement caused by the illness and death of my beloved wife God gave me a verse that greatly strengthened me, and I have taken this promise as a source of strength for the duration of my life. It is found in Psalm 27:1, "*The Lord is my light and my salvation: whom shall I fear? the Lord is the strength of my life; of whom shall I be afraid*?" In my mind I picture a strong oak tree standing alone in a field. It has been struck by many a storm, but though twisted and gnarled it stands as a monument of power and durability. I look closer and I view a small fragile vine winding its way up and around the strong oak. We are weak and none of us can live the sanctified life in our own strength, but as the vine finds security in the tree, so we can say with Paul "*I can do all things through Christ which strengtheneth me*" (Philippians 4:13).

Sing unto the Lord
(Psalm 30:4a)

Help me to watch and pray,
And on Thyself rely.
Assured if I my trust betray
I shall forever die.
—Charles Wesley[1]

Verse to Memorize: *For we are made partakers of Christ, if we hold the beginning of our confidence steadfast unto the end . . .* (Hebrews 3:14).

Saved from Despair

Background Scripture: II Samuel 11-12:1-23

***But now he is dead, wherefore should I fast? Can I bring him back again? I shall go to him, but he shall not return to me* (II Samuel 12:23).**

David paid an awful price for a moment of folly. In Proverbs 20:17 we read, "*Bread of deceit is sweet to a man; but afterwards his mouth shall be filled with gravel.*" Sin always looks different after it has been committed. The child born to him as a result of his sin with Bathsheba, the wife of Uriah, must die. We read, *"Howbeit, because by this deed thou hast given great occasion to the enemies of the Lord to blaspheme, the child also born unto thee shall surely die*" (II Samuel 12:14). When one sins he does not suffer alone. Many times the innocent suffer as in this account.

David humbled himself before God and fasted hoping God would reverse the sentence, But the child still died. His servants feared to tell him of his son's death. But as the "*servants whispered, David perceived that the child was dead: therefore David said unto his servants, Is the child dead? And they said, He is dead*" (II Samuel 12:19b).

Is there hope for one who has fallen as low as King David did on this occasion? The individual who has fallen into sin can despair like Judas Iscariot or repent as we read in the account of David's prayer and restoration in Psalm 51. In that prayer David prays to be restored, but he realized he had a further need of a clean heart. He prays, "*Create in me a clean heart, O God; and renew a right spirit within me* (Psalm 51:10).

King David had learned his lesson the hard way, but now sets out for a new beginning. After the child's death he took care of the practical cares as he "*arose from the earth, and washed, and anointed himself, and changed his apparel, and came into the house of the Lord, and worshipped: then he came to his own house; and when he required, they set bread before him, and he did eat"* (II Samuel 12:20b). Life must go on even in the hardest of circumstances, and so it did with David, but under new management.

After thoroughly repenting and asking God for a clean heart and having made all amends as far as possible one should leave the past sins and failures where God has placed them in the depths of the sea as we read in Micah 7:19. "*He will turn again, He will have compassion upon us; He will subdue our iniquities; and Thou wilt cast all their sins into the depths of the sea.*" We cannot be at our best for God and His Kingdom today if we continue to brood over past sins and failures that are covered by the blood. As the past comes into focus it should remind us of the price paid for our redemption and cause us to humble ourselves before God, and with St. Paul cry out, "*Thanks be unto God for His unspeakable gift*" (II Corinthians 9:15). Yes, there is a new start for those who sincerely turn back to God as David did and find that life can still have meaning.

Sing Unto The Lord
(Psalm 30:4a)

Once in sins darkest night I was wandering alone;
A stranger to mercy I stood.
But the Saviour came nigh when He heard my faint cry,
And He put my sins under the blood.[1]

Verse to Memorize: *If we confess our sins, He is faithful and just to forgive us our sins, and to cleanse us from all unrighteousness* (I John 1:9).

Solomon's Fringe Benefits

Background Scripture: I Kings 3:5-15

***And I have also given thee that which thou hast not asked, both riches, and honour: so that there shall not be any among the kings like unto thee all thy days* (I Kings 3:13).**

When one seeks employment he is not only interested in the salary but is concerned about the fringe benefits, or of that which is of value beyond the specified remuneration. "*In Gibeon the Lord appeared to Solomon in a dream by night: and God said, Ask what I shall give thee*" (I Kings 3:5). Solomon's request was not for personal selfish goals and ambitions, but for wisdom as king to lead God's people. This prayer so pleased God that He not only gave him wisdom, but many fringe benefits as we see in verses 13-14. "*And I have also given thee that which thou hast not asked, both riches, and honour: so that there shall not be any among the kings like unto thee all thy days. And if thou wilt walk in my ways, to keep my commandments, as thy father David did walk, then I will lengthen thy days.*"

Not only did God give Solomon the privilege of requesting in prayer what he desired, but our Lord grants the same favor to all His children, for we read what Jesus says, "*Ask and it shall be given you…*" (Matthew 7:7a). However, as in Solomon's prayer the petition must not be motivated by selfish or personal gain, but by that which is in God's will and which will glorify Him. James states, "*Ye ask, and receive not, because ye ask amiss, that ye may consume it upon your lusts*" (James 4:3). In that case God cannot honor the request, but when the desire is from pure motives and to God's glory He will answer the same as He did for Solomon and even give more than requested. Haven't we all as His children found it so in our walk with Him? David writes, "*Blessed be the Lord, who daily loadeth us with benefits, even the God of our salvation. Selah*" (Psalm 68-19). Even as earthly parents find pleasure in giving to their children, so God our heavenly Father takes pleasure in those who are fully yielded to His will. Paul tells us, *"But as it is written, Eye hath not seen, nor ear heard, neither have entered into the heart of man, the things which God hath prepared for them that love Him"* (I Corinthians 2:9).

Sing unto the Lord (Psalm 30:4a)

And I have brought to thee,
Down from my home above,
Salvation full and free,
My pardon and my love.
I bring, I bring rich gifts to thee.
What hast thou brought to me?
I bring, I bring rich gifts to thee.
What hast thou brought to me?[1]

Verse to Memorize: *But seek ye first the kingdom of God, and His righteousness; and all these things shall be added unto you* (Matthew 6:33).

Faith When Life Tumbles In

Background Scripture: II Kings 4:8-37

...Is it well with thee?Is it well with thy husband?Is it well with thy child? And she answered, It is well **(II Kings 4:26b).**

In his frequent journeys to Shunem, the prophet Elisha passed by the home of a great woman who was solicitous of the prophet's welfare. This good lady fed the prophet as often as he passed by and in due time consults with her husband as to what further aid they could furnish him. She perceived that Elisha was a holy man of God and suggested to her husband that they provide, "*...a little chamber...on the wall, and let us set for him there a bed, and a table, and a stool, and a candlestick: and it shall be, when he cometh to us, that he shall turn in thither*" (II Kings 4:10).

In appreciation for her hospitality the prophet desires to return the favor but seems to be at a loss as to what would be the appropriate thing to do. When asked if she would like to have a recommendation to the king or captain of the host on her behalf, "*she answered, I dwell among mine own people.*" In other words she said, I am content with my lot in life. Elisha insisted on doing something for her as a reward for all her care, so in consultation with Gehazi, his servant, it was decided God would give her a son. But the son became sick and, despite her tender care, he died. This good mother of great faith knew what course to take and naturally turned to God in her despair. She went to the man of God, and while at a distance Elisha sent Gehazi and told him to ask of her welfare with three questions; "*Is it well with thee? is it well with thy husband?Is it well with the child? And she answered, It is well*" (II Kings 4:26b).

There is a "fair weather" kind of faith that can be exercised when things are going well, and we can see the end of the tunnel, but it takes great faith when the prognosis is terminal. Many of us know what it is to see members of our family suffer and die. But in life there are various difficult problems, but so long as we keep our trust and faith in God we can still say, "*It is well*" with my soul, and find an anchor both steadfast and sure.

Many of our hymns have been born out of an experience of suffering. It was such an experience that gave birth to the hymn, "It Is Well with My Soul." Horatio G. Spafford, though crushed after receiving a telegram of the loss of his family at sea, penned the words of this consoling hymn.

We as humans are limited in our capacity to bring comfort to storm tossed souls, but the Holy Spirit, the promised Comforter, can bring relief and solace where the pain is too deep and beyond reach of all human resources. This source of strength is available to all of God's children who call upon Him in faith believing.

Sing Unto The Lord
(Psalm 30-4a)

When peace like a river attendeth my way,
When sorrows like sea billows roll,
Whatever my lot, Thou hast taught me to say,
"It is well, it is well with my soul."[1]

Verse to Memorize: *When thou passest through the waters, I will be with thee; and through the rivers, they shall not overflow thee: When thou walkest through the fire, thou shalt not be burned; neither shall the flame kindle upon thee. For I am the Lord thy God, The Holy One of Israel, the Saviour* (Isaiah 43:2-3a).

PRAYER THAT PLEASES GOD

Background Scripture: I Chronicles 4:9-10

***And Jabez called on the God of Israel, saying, Oh, that thou wouldest bless me indeed, and enlarge my coast, and that thine hand might be with me, and that thou wouldest keep me from evil, that it may not grieve me! And God granted him that which he requested* (I Chronicles 4:10).**

In the midst of a long list of genealogies we find a little gold nugget in verse 10. What was it that caused the inspired writer to take time out and give us an account of the prayer of this good man named Jabez?

In verse nine we find "*his mother called his name Jabez, saying, because I bare him with sorrow*" (I Chronicles 4:9b). But subsequent events, no doubt, proved to his mother and all people that he had been wrongfully named, for in time Jabez brought joy to his mother, and to many others. It reminds us of what Jesus said when conveying a spiritual truth by way of teaching how, "*A woman when she is in travail hath sorrow, because her hour is come: but as soon as she is delivered of the child, she remembereth no more the anguish, for joy that a man is born into the world*" (St. John 16:21).

The Scripture gives us a very brief account of the birth and life of Jabez, but enough is recorded to reveal his character. Here we find an unselfish prayer all for God's glory. He wants God to help him in all areas of his life including his business concerns, or what we would commonly call his secular life as he prays, "*...Oh, that thou wouldest bless me indeed, and enlarge my coast...*" verse 10. In order to reach this goal, Jabez felt his dependence on God, and asked that God's hand might be with him, and keep him from evil. Jabez was aware of the devastating effect of sin. He realized the truth stated in Job 31:3, "*Is not destruction to the wicked? And a strange punishment to the workers of iniquity*?"

This follower of God wanted his Lord's blessing on every detail of his life. He not only requested that God would enlarge his coast but he asked for spiritual blessings that God's hand would be with him and keep him from evil. God is interested in the whole man with all our needs both temporal and spiritual, and will answer and meet these needs when we ask for those things that pleases Him in the spirit that Jabez prayed, for we read, "*And God granted him that which he requested*" (I Chronicles 4:10b).

Sing unto the Lord
(Psalm 30:4a)

Would you live for Jesus, and be always pure and good?
Would you walk with him within the narrow road?
Would you have Him bear your burden, carry all your load?
Let Him have His way with thee.[1]

Verse to Memorize: *As righteousness tendeth to life: so he that pursueth evil pursueth to his own death* (Proverbs 11:19).

The Price of a Revival

***If my people, which are called by my name, shall humble themselves, and pray, and seek my face, and turn from their wicked ways: then will I hear from heaven, and will forgive their sin, and will heal their land* (II Chronicles 7:14).**

Revival always begins with God's people. The norm for a Christian is to live a life free from sin, properly understood. In making this statement I am using the definition of John Wesley as he said, "sin is a willful transgression of a known law of God." I am not referring to all the mistakes, human frailties, and weaknesses to which all in this state of probation are subject to. King David distinguished between mistakes and willful sin in Psalm 19:3 where we read, "*Keep back thy servant from presumptuous sins; let them not have dominion over me: then I shall be upright, and I shall be innocent from the great transgressions*." With this distinction in mind we see how God has made provision through our Lord and Saviour Jesus Christ that we can live above sin in this present sinful world. In Hebrews 13:12 we read, "*Wherefore Jesus also, that He might sanctify the people with His own blood, suffered without the gate*." Not only did God make provision for us to live a holy life, but also in His high priestly prayer Jesus prayed for us that we might be enabled to live such a life. Listen to His prayer: "*I pray not that Thou shouldest take them out of the world, but that Thou shouldest keep them from the evil*" (St. John 17:15). But someone may say that doesn't include me in this present modern sinful world. Again, listen to Jesus as He continues to pray, "*Neither pray I for these alone, but for them also which shall believe on me through their word*" (St. John 17:20). That prayer includes you and me. So we see there is no excuse for living in sin.

While the ideal is that we "*might serve Him without fear, In holiness and righteousness before Him all the days of our life*" as we read in Luke 1:74b-75, yet, we must take people where they are and realize there are those who fall short of the ideal and need to be restored.

There is a danger of sinning and then trying to cover it up by saying it was a mistake. The correct course would be to plead the blood of Christ and be restored in His image. The holy man of God never plans on falling from the grace of God, but if through lack of watchfulness he should be so unfortunate as to fail God, yet, there is provision for his recovery and his restoration. We read, "*My little children, these things write I unto you, that ye sin not. And if any man sin, we have an Advocate with the Father, Jesus Christ the righteous: And He is the propitiation for our sins: and not for ours only, but also for the sins of the whole world*" (I John 2:1-2). I heard Dr. W. T. Purkiser once say that the Christian life is like driving your automobile on a journey. You don't expect to have a flat tire, but it is good to have an extra tire with you in case you do. The Christian does not expect to fall into sin or plan to follow such a course, but we can be thankful provision has been made through Christ that we have an Advocate and can be restored through Christ's shed blood, and like Peter can still be a blessing to the Kingdom of God.

We see how genuine humility, prayer, and seeking God's face with true repentance will bring revival in this our day.

Sing unto the Lord (Psalm 30:4a)

Search me, O God, and know my heart today.
Try me, O Saviour; know my thoughts, I pray.
See if there be some wicked way in me;
Cleanse me from every sin, and set me free.[1]

Verse to Memorize: *Wilt Thou not revive us again: that Thy people may rejoice in Thee?* (Psalm 85:6)

A Time to Rejoice

Background Scripture: Ezra 2:68-70; 3:1-13

But many of the priests and Levites and chief of the fathers, who were ancient men that had seen the first house, when the foundation of this house was laid before their eyes, wept with a loud voice; and many shouted for joy: So that the people could not discern the noise of the shout of joy from the noise of the weeping of the people: for the people shouted with a loud shout, and the noise was heard from afar off (Ezra 3:12-13).

Emotions ran high as the foundation of this second house was being laid. We do not know all that was going through the minds of this people that caused some to weep and others to shout. We can only conjecture as to what they were thinking as they viewed this project. However, we do know tears can be an expression of joy even in time of sorrow.

These ancient priests, Levites and chief of the fathers may have been present for the dedication of the first temple and remembered how God's presence was manifest on that occasion. We read the account of that dedication in I Kings 8:10-11, "*And it came to pass, when the priests were come out of the holy place, that the cloud filled the house of the Lord, So that the priests could not stand to minister because of the cloud: for the glory of the Lord had filled the house of the Lord.*"

In that case these ancient leaders could be wondering if it would happen again after this manner in the new temple now under construction. God does not change, and we can experience the blessing of God in any age or place when the required conditions are met. Listen to God's word. "*Jesus Christ the same yesterday, and today, and forever*" (Hebrews 13:8). In fact the prophet Haggai writes, "*The glory of the latter house shall be greater than of the former, saith the Lord of hosts*" (Haggai 2:9a). There is no retreat in serving God, but a forward march to meet the new challenges that lie before us.

There are those who find it difficult to separate the building that houses the church from the real church or bride of Christ, which consists of redeemed souls. When this happens, progress is impeded and the Kingdom of God suffers loss. Naturally there is sentiment attached to things and places where God met us, but we should not permit overly sentimental feelings to hinder God's working in and through us today. This was exactly what happened to Israel when they worshipped the brazen serpent, the symbol instead of God himself. In recounting the reforms that King Hezekiah made, it is related that, "*He removed the high places, and brake the images, and cut down the groves, and brake in pieces the brazen serpent that Moses had made: for unto those days the children of Israel did burn incense to it: and he called it Nehushtan*" (II Kings 18:4).

Jesus said to the woman at the well, "*Woman, believe me, the hour cometh, when ye shall neither in this mountain, nor yet at Jerusalem, worship the Father*" (St. John 4:21b). "*But the hour cometh, and now is, when the true worshippers shall worship the Father in spirit and in truth: for the Father seeketh such to worship Him*" (St, John 4:23).

On this occasion of rebuilding the temple, God's people rejoiced whether by shouting or weeping, and so should we rejoice. St. Paul writes, "*Rejoice in the Lord always: and again I say, Rejoice*" (Philippians 4:4). So whether in an old building or new let us live so close to God that the fire will never go out! Dr. J.B. Chapman, late General Superintendent of the Church of the Nazarene, said when one is born in the fire he is not satisfied with the smoke, I say, "Amen!"

Sing unto the Lord
(Psalm 30:4a)

Rejoice, ye pure in heart;
Rejoice, give thanks, and sing.
Your festal banner wave on high,
The Cross of Christ, your King.[1]

Verse to Memorize: *Rejoice in the Lord, O ye righteous: for praise is comely for the upright* (Psalm 33:1).

The Sacredness of Work

Background Scripture: Nehemiah 1-4:6

***So built we the wall; and all the wall was joined together unto the half thereof: for the people had a mind to work* (Nehemiah 4:6).**

Today is Labor Day in the year 2000. This is the day we honor and pay tribute to all workingmen and women. Not only do men honor and respect the workingmen and women, but also God has placed His blessing and badge of approval on honest dedicated work done for His glory and honor. We see this as God called men and women in the building and furnishing of the tabernacle. We read in Exodus 31:1-3, "*And the Lord spake unto Moses, saying, See I have called by name Bezaleel the son of Uri, the son of Hur, of the tribe of Judah: And I have filled him with the Spirit of God, in wisdom, and in understanding, and in knowledge, and in all manner of workmanship.*" Here was a man who had all his skill and talents surrendered completely to the will of God. Bezaleel was so filled with the Spirit of God, that he did his ordinary work as a sacrament to the Lord. However menial our task, when we do it with an eye single to His glory, it is transformed from the secular work to that which is spiritual. Our blessed Lord and Savior Jesus Christ at the age of twelve was as much in the will of His Father "*sitting in the midst of the doctors, both hearing them, and asking them questions*" (Luke 2:46b) or working as a carpenter, as He was when He faced the cross in Gethsemane and cried out to His Father, "*O my Father, if it be possible, let this cup pass from me: nevertheless not as I will, but as Thou wilt*" (Matthew 26:39b).

As we go about our work, let us heed what St. Paul wrote to the Colossians, "*And whatsoever ye do, do it heartily, as to the Lord, and not unto men; Knowing that of the Lord ye shall receive the reward of the inheritance: for ye serve the Lord Christ" (Colossians 3:23-24).*

A mistake men repeatedly make is in thinking work in itself is the result of the curse placed upon the ground, (Genesis 3:17) and the resultant suffering that comes upon men as they toil for a living. Before the fall God mentions in Genesis 2:5b, "*and there was not a man to till the ground.*" The inference is that God expected man to toil and work in the garden. The truth is that work would have been free from the curse placed upon the ground, if man had not sinned in disobedience to God, but he would still have had work. Yet, we can still enjoy the pleasure of work as God originally intended for mankind even with the penalty attached to labor because of the fall. There is the satisfaction of looking on work well done and feel as God felt after Creation as we read in Genesis 1:31(part), "*...And, behold, it was very good.*"

We see the sacredness of work as we read about the creative activity of God. In Genesis 2:2 it is recorded, "*And on the seventh day God ended His work which He had made; and He rested on the seventh day from all His work which He had made.*" Jesus gave us an example of the necessity of labor when he said, "*I must work the work of Him that sent me, while it is day: the night cometh, when no man can work*" (St. John 9:4). So we conclude if we are followers of Christ who "*leaving us an example, that ye should follow His steps,*" (I Peter 2:21b) then He will be our model when it comes to our labor as in all other areas of our lives.

Heaven will not be an abode of idleness, and in our spiritual bodies we will never become weary in our work. That land will be a place of much activity, which will be suited to our eternal happiness as we join the angels as they proclaim, "*Holy, holy, holy, is the Lord of hosts*" (Isaiah 6:3a). In the meanwhile let us be faithful to our talents and the work God has assigned us during this time of our probation on earth that we may hear the Master say, "*Well done, thou good and faithful servant thou hast been faithful over a few things, I will make thee ruler over many things: enter thou into the joy of thy Lord*" (Matthew 25:23b).

Sing unto the Lord
(Psalm 30:4a)

Work for the night is coming. Work thro' the sunny noon.
Fill brightest hours with labor: Rest comes sure and soon.
Give every flying minute, Something to keep in store.
Work for the night is coming, When man works no more.[1]

Verse to Memorize: *Yea, a man may say, Thou hast faith, and I have works: shew me thy faith without thy works, and I will shew thee my faith by my works* (James 2:18).

Vicarious Sacrifice

Background Scripture: Esther 3-4

***Go gather together all the Jews that are present in Shushan, and fast ye for me, and neither eat or drink three days, night or day: I also and my maidens will fast likewise; and so will I go in unto the king, which is not according to the law: and if I perish, I perish* (Esther 4:16).**

Queen Esther is a classical example of vicarious sacrifice. If necessary she was willing to die in order to save her people from annihilation.

There are other Biblical characters who put their "lives on the line" and were willing to pay the supreme sacrifice for the sake of God and His kingdom if necessary. I mention just two of the many. When Israel sinned against God, we read of Moses interceding for the nation in Exodus 32:31-32. "*And Moses returned unto the Lord, and said, Oh, this people have sinned a great sin, and have made them gods of gold. Yet now, if Thou wilt forgive their sin—; and if not, blot me, I pray thee, out of thy book which thou hast written.*" Then we find St. Paul in the New Testament expressing the same sentiment when burdened for the salvation of the Jews, his fellow kinsmen, in Romans 9:2-3, "*That I have great heaviness and continual sorrow in my heart. For I could wish that myself were accursed from Christ for my brethren, my kinsmen according to the flesh:*" The greatest example of vicarious sacrifice and suffering is our blessed Lord and Saviour Jesus Christ. We read in Philippians 2:8, "*And being found in fashion* as *a man, He humbled Himself, and became obedient unto death, even the death of the cross.*"

There are people in our day who sacrifice their lives for the sake of others. In time of war that soldier who gives his life in protecting his "buddy," that mother who enters a house on fire to save her child and in so doing loses her own life, or that one who works under hazardous conditions shortening his or her own life in order to provide comforts that we enjoy, are all examples of vicarious sacrifice.

There was no easy solution for the dilemma that the Jews faced during the time when Esther reigned as queen. Queen Esther was the key figure, and it could have cost her life to take her stand for the Jewish nation. Any person who entered the inner court who was not called was put to death except that the king should hold out the golden scepter. Esther had no assurance that the king would accept her, and finally she becomes decisive and asks for prayer and fasting on her behalf, and she goes against the law in order to save her people. She then cries out, "*...and if I perish, I perish*" (Esther 4:16b).

Jesus does not mince words as to the cost of discipleship. In Matthew 16:24b Jesus says, *"If any man will come after me, Let him deny himself and take up his cross, and follow me"*"" This means it will cost all you have including one's life if necessary to be a genuine disciple of Christ.

God is in search of helpers as He was in the time of Ezekiel. There we read, "*And I sought for a man among them, that should make up the hedge, and stand in the gap before me for the land, that I should not destroy it: but I found none*" (Ezekiel 22:30). Queen Esther stood in the gap. Mordecai in conveying the message to Esther said, "*...And who knoweth whether thou art come to the kingdom for such a time as this*?" (Esther 4:14b). We all have a gap to fill as we labor in earth's over ripened harvest. The cost may mean much sacrifice, but the reward far outweighs the cost, for God's word says, "*...godliness is profitable unto all things, having promise of the life that now is, and of that which is to come.*"

Sing unto the Lord
(Psalm 30:4a)

Must Jesus bear the cross alone,
And all the world go free?
No, there's a cross for everyone,
And there's a cross for me.[1]

Verse to Memorize: *And whosoever doth not bear his cross, and come after me, cannot be my disciple* (Luke 14:27).

Job

Suffering Within the Will of God

Background Scripture: Book of Job

***Then Job arose, and rent his mantle, and shaved his head, and fell down upon the ground, and worshipped, And said, Naked came I out of my mother's womb, and naked shall I return thither: the Lord gave, and the Lord taketh away; blessed be the name of the Lord* (Job 1:20-21).**

The question as to why the righteous suffer, and the sinner seemingly suffers less than God-fearing men and women is as modern as it is ancient. This thought troubled Job as he rehearses it in Job 21:7-15; then in the verses following Job sees that the triumph of the wicked is of short duration. In Psalm 73 the Psalmist is faced with the same difficulty, and arrives at the same conclusion as Job. In fact this thought almost caused the Psalmist to backslide as he testifies in verses two and three of this Psalm. "*But as for me, my feet were almost gone; my steps had well nigh slipped. For I was envious at the foolish when I saw the prosperity of the wicked.*" The thought was too painful for him "*until I went into the sanctuary of God; then understood I their end*" (Psalm 73:17). He then came to realize his view of this problem was too short-sighted, and all the inequalities of this life will be settled if given time. An illustration is recorded that points out this truth. "An infidel published the statement that he had an acre of Sunday corn which was the best in the community. He said that he broke the ground on Sunday, planted the corn on Sunday, plowed it only on Sunday, and that it was the finest in the neighborhood. By the middle of October he would have it harvested and safe in the crib. This was done on Sunday. He was ridiculing the idea of there being a God and declared his success in this matter proved it. As he was thus boasting and defying God to one of his Christian neighbors, the neighbor quietly replied, "Yes, but God does not always square accounts with mankind by the middle of October."[1] It was so in the account of the rich man and Lazarus as we read in St.Luke 16:25, "*But Abraham said, Son, remember that thou in thy lifetime receivedst thy good things, and likewise Lazarus evil things: but now he is comforted, and thou art tormented.*"

In his suffering Job rises above it all and the Holy Spirit enabled him before the death and resurrection of our Lord and Savior Jesus Christ to declare some of the most sublime truth found in God's word concerning the life to come for God's people in the next and better world to come where Job cries out, "*Oh that my words were now written! Oh that they were printed in a book! That they were graven with an iron pen and lead in the rock forever! For I know that my Redeemer liveth, and that He shall stand at the latter day upon the earth: and though after my skin worms destroy this body, yet in my flesh shall I see God: Whom I shall see for myself, and mine eyes shall behold, and not another; though my reins be consumed within me*" (Job 19:23-27). Job in effect is saying let the worse come upon me in this life, yet all is well if I retain my integrity and make it through to heaven and see Jesus.

There is a truth found in Job 42:10a that should be a source of comfort and strength for all who sorrow when it is put into practice. It states, "*And the Lord turned the captivity of Job, when he prayed for his friends*:" We always feel better when we focus on the needs of others and pray for them. In doing this Job found what we all can experience, and that is our depression and gloom can be alleviated as we trust God and turn away from our own self-centeredness in meeting the needs of others.

The end result or the bottom line is what God sees in our spiritual development during our probation on earth. Satan seeks to destroy God's people for we read, "*Be sober, be vigilant;* because *your adversary the devil, as a roaring lion walketh about seeking whom he may devour*" (I Peter 5:8). But God uses and turns these times of testing to draw us closer to Him, and to strengthen us in the faith. After having passed through this long "dark night of the soul" Job testifies, "*I have heard of thee by the hearing of the ear: but now mine eye seeth thee*" (Job 42:5).

Sing unto the Lord
(Psalm 30:4a)

Under His wings I am safely abiding.
Tho' the night deepens and tempests are wild,
Still I can trust Him; I know He will keep me.
He has redeemed me, and I am His child.[2]

Verse to Memorize: *Be still, and know that I am God: I will be exalted among the heathen, I will be exalted in the earth* (Psalm 46:10).

The Resolute Heart

Background Scripture: Psalm 112:1-10

***He shall not be afraid of evil tidings: his heart is fixed, trusting in the Lord* (Psalm 112:7).**

God is never caught off guard as to the providential circumstances and happenings we experience in our lives here on earth. He has plans for us as individuals from all eternity. God *told the prophet Jeremiah, "Before I formed thee in the belly I knew thee; and before thou camest forth out of the womb I sanctified thee, and I ordained thee a prophet unto the nations*" (Jeremiah 1:5). As with the prophet even so God has a blueprint for the life of each individual.

Jesus tells us that a sparrow "*shall not fall on the ground without your Father*" (Matthew 10:29b). It took two sparrows to equal the value of the smallest coin then in usage, yet our Saviour says not one shall fall without God's care. So why should we be so solicitous concerning the events or evil tidings that we may experience in the course of our living when our "*heart is fixed, trusting in the Lord.*" In Isaiah 40:27-31, the prophet explains how our way is not hid from the Lord.

The God-fearing man stands firm during stressful times because his heart is fixed, trusting in the Lord. In order to have a fixed heart it is basic that the heart be cleansed from all sin by the precious blood of our Lord Jesus Christ, for we cannot have victory by merely a set of the will. Still, even in those who have experienced the highest attainments of grace, it is necessary to burn all bridges behind us, and have it settled in our heart and mind the course we will take. I well remember during the Cuban missile crisis how the late President John F. Kennedy made it clear to the Soviet Union that the ships carrying missiles and already on their way to Cuba would be warned by shooting over the ships, and would then be sunk if they proceeded. Fortunately, they turned back and war was avoided. We must have the same fixed determination in our spiritual warfare against Satan and his forces. James writes, "*Submit yourselves therefore to God. Resist the devil, and he will flee from you*" (James 4:7).

A good man made the statement to me that a man does not know what he would do if he were to face a certain temptation. Unless one has it already settled in his heart and mind that there will be no turning back, the chances are he will go down in defeat, and become another casualty in this spiritual warfare in which we are all engaged.

Not only must we have a fixed heart, but also we must have a trusting heart. We will not always understand the way God is leading. Space does not permit me to give all the Biblical and personal illustrations, but suffice it to say we are safe if God is in the lead. We must learn to trust God, for there is an element of trust in genuine faith. Evangelist C.W. Ruth told a story that forcibly illustrates this truth. He said "a few years ago a man walked a wire rope across the gorge at Niagara Falls. After this feat was successfully performed, it was reported that he would push a man across the gorge in a wheelbarrow the following day. This caused much excitement. The papers had glaring headlines. Few seemed to think that it could be done, while many argued that this would be an impossible feat. Mr. Ruth presented himself on the streets of Niagara Falls the day of the proposed performance, freely expressing his belief that the ropewalker would take his man across successfully. Just at this time the ropewalker came along the street, meeting Mr. Ruth. 'I'm certainly glad to meet you,' said Mr. Ruth, as they shook hands, 'I have been boosting for you all day. I believe you know your business; I say you'll take your man across safely.' 'It is indeed a pleasure to meet you, Mr. Ruth,' replied the man, 'I've been looking all day for a man like you, I want you to get into the wheelbarrow.'"[1] Just so we must trust God's care and leadership as we travel this rough road of life. God has never lost one soul who has fully trusted Him. "*Trust in the Lord with all thine heart, and lean not unto thine own understanding*" (Proverbs 3:5).

Sing unto the Lord (Psalm 30:4a)

How firm a foundation, ye saints of the Lord,
Is laid for your faith in His excellent Word!
What more can He say than to you He hath said,
To you who for refuge to Jesus have fled?[2]

Verse to Memorize: *God is our refuge and strength, a very present help in trouble* (Psalm 46:1).

A Better Way to Combat Evil

***A soft answer turneth away wrath: but grievous words stir up anger* (Proverbs 15:1).**

There is dynamite in the word softly spoken. In another scripture in Proverbs 25:15 we read, "*By long forbearing is a prince persuaded, and a soft tongue breaketh the bone.*" This truth is contrary to popular opinion, nevertheless the truth remains, because it is founded on God's eternal word, and it is proven in everyday practical experience.

Who is not touched deeply with the soft, yet firm words of our Saviour when Judas Iscariot betrayed Him with a kiss? Jesus said, "*Friend, wherefore art thou come*?" (Matthew 26:50). Again in verse 55b, "*Are ye come out as against a thief with swords and staves for to take me*?" Get quiet before God, and listen closely to Christ's praying for a lost world as He faced death on a cruel cross, "*Father, forgive them; for they know not what they do*" (Luke 23:34).

These words are not weak coming from one conquered by the enemy, but from the Messiah, about whom St. John records, "*All things were made by Him; and without Him was not anything made that was made*" (St. John 1:3) and testified as He faced death; "*Thinkest thou that I cannot now pray to my Father, and He shall presently give me more than twelve legions of angels*?" (Matthew 26:53). These words of Christ were powerful.

On one occasion when the chief priests and Pharisees questioned the officers as to why they had not brought Jesus, all they could say was, "*Never man spake like this man*" (St. John 7:46b). His words were soft but with authority.

Is there not a lesson here for us as followers of Christ, "*who leaving us an example, that ye should follow His steps*"? (I Peter 2:21b) It must be a voluntary response. St. Paul writes, *Now I Paul myself beseech you by the meekness and gentleness of Christ...*" (II Corinthians 10:1a). May Christ be our example in this area of our lives as in our entire walk with Him.

King Solomon reminds us, "*Where no wood is, there the fire goeth out*" (Proverbs 26:20a). We are taking this truth somewhat out of context in applying it here as it refers to a talebearer, but we are doing no injustice to the text in using it with reference to the tone of our conversation, for harsh words only call for more fiery words. We can put the fire out as we dampen them with kind and soft words. This is the better way to combat evil, by following our Lord and Saviour Jesus Christ, "*who, when He was reviled, reviled not again; when He suffered, He threatened not; but committed Himself to Him that judgeth righteously*" (I Peter 2:23).

Sing unto the Lord
(Psalm 30:4a)

Sing them over again to me,
Wonderful words of Life!
Let me more of their beauty see,
Wonderful words of Life![1]

Verse to Memorize: *Let your speech, be always with grace, seasoned with salt, that ye may know how ye ought to answer every man* (Colossians 4:6).

A Wise Conclusion

***Let us hear the conclusion of the whole matter: Fear God, and keep His commandments: for this is the whole duty of man* (Ecclesiastes 12:13).**

In this book of Ecclesiastes we read, "*Vanity of vanities, saith the Preacher, vanities of vanities; all is vanity*" (Ecclesiastes 1:2). The word vanity in all of its forms is recorded thirty-seven times in the twelve chapters of this book. Why? It is because King Solomon came to the conclusion, as all men eventually do, that genuine happiness and satisfaction are not to be found in the temporal and fleeting pleasures of this world, for to man created in the image of God, peace and satisfaction comes only when the soul is in right relationship with its Maker. Jesus in rebuking Satan said, "*Man shall not live by bread alone, but by every word that proceedeth out of the mouth of the God*" (Matthew 4:4b).

In a very scientific way, King Solomon proceeds to discover the secret of happiness while living on earth. He said, "*And I gave my heart to seek and search out by wisdom concerning all things that are done under heaven*" (Ecclesiastes 1:13a). Solomon could have reached his conclusion more quickly if he had approached God in faith rather than by the avenue of wisdom, for… "*the world by wisdom knew not God*" (I Corinthians 1:21).

In his search for happiness, Solomon tried many things that men usually think will cause one to be content and happy, only to find vanity and disappointment.

Notice his experiment as we read through this book. He tries; mirth (2:7), wine(2:3), great works (2:4-6), servants (2:7), silver and gold (2:8), singers and musical instruments (2:8), all his eyes desired (2:10). After trying out these the wise man says, "*Then I looked on all the works that my hands had wrought, and on the labour that I had laboured to do: and, behold, all was vanity and vexation of spirit, and there was no profit under the sun*" (Ecclesiastes 2:11).

After his experiment he reaches a conclusion and says, "*Fear*

God, and keep His commandments: for this is the whole duty of man" (Ecclesiastes 12:13b).

After being saved out of a life lived in deep sin, St. Augustine testified to the fact that God created us for Himself and our souls are restless until they rest in Him.

Why should mankind go on a search for happiness when King Solomon already has proved that only God can fill the vacuum that exists in every unregenerate heart? Jesus invites all to come, saying, "*Come unto me, all ye that labour and are heavy laden, and I will give you rest*" (Matthew 11:28).

Sing unto the Lord
(Psalm 30:4a)

Hallelujah! I have found Him—
Whom my soul so long has craved!
Jesus satisfies my longings;
Thro' His blood I now am saved.[1]

Verse to Memorize: *For what is a man profited, if he shall gain the whole world, and lose his own soul? or what shall a man give in exchange for his soul?* (Matthew 16:26)

OUR FIRST PRIORITY

***...They made me the keeper of the vineyards; but mine own vineyard have I not kept* (Song of Solomon 1:6b).**

Dr. Hardy C. Powers, late General Superintendent of the Church of the Nazarene, was visiting in a foreign country on a missionary assignment. As part of his work, he was giving a test to native ministers. One of the questions asked was, "What is the first duty of a General Superintendent?" Dr. Powers was impressed by the answer of one ministerial student. He answered, "The first duty of a General Superintendent is to save his own soul." While the answer was not correct as far as the duties of a General Superintendent as outlined in the manual of the denomination, yet in the light of eternity it could not have been truer.

Here in the text is a girl who was made a keeper of vineyards but failed to cultivate her own vineyard. There are different interpretations as to the theological significance of this scripture and its meaning, but it can be applied to our own stewardship in serving God and do no injustice to the truth found in the text.

Time is never wasted in cultivating our spiritual experience. David prayed saying, "*Search me, O God, and know my heart: try me, and know my thoughts: and see if there be any wicked way in me, and lead me in the way everlasting*" (Psalm 139:23-24). Paul exhorts the Corinthians saying, "*Examine yourselves, whether ye be in the faith*;" (II Corinthians 13:5)

There is a morbid introverted self-inspection that is not healthy. Someone has stated that to every look at self we should take ten looks at Jesus. In growing a plant it would not be the correct thing to do to constantly pull it from the soil and inspect its root to see if it is still healthy. So we can be overly self-centered.

But if we are going to be useful in building God's kingdom, and save our souls, we must take time to be holy. There is an interesting scripture full of truth found in Ecclesiastes 10:10 that reads, "*If the iron be blunt, and he do not whet the edge, then must he put to more strength: but wisdom is profitable to direct.*" When the church fails to keep "the keen edge," then invariably she resorts to a multiplication of human manipulation in order to see church growth. We can increase in numbers without having the blessing of God.

But the church remains spiritual only as each individual cultivates his or her spiritual experience. Even as great a saint as Paul found it necessary to be on guard as to his continued personal relationship with his Lord and Master. He writes, "*But I keep under my body, and bring it into subjection: lest that by any means, when I have preached to others, I myself should be a castaway*" (I Corinthians 9:27).

When a church loses ground spiritually, it is not a time to become discouraged and critical, but a time to humble ourselves before God and pray for a revival according to II Chronicles 7:14, "*If my people, which are called by my name, shall humble themselves, and pray, and seek my face, and turn* sin, *and will heal their land from their wicked ways; then will I hear from heaven, and will forgive their sin.*"

May each of us resolve to keep our spiritual vineyard, and see revival in this our day. May God help us in this endeavor.

Sing unto the Lord
(Psalm 30:4a) *Take time to be holy. The world rushes on;*
Spend much time in secret with Jesus alone.
By looking to Jesus, Like Him thou shalt be;
Thy friends in thy conduct His likeness shall see.[1]

Verse to Memorize: *Now when they saw the boldness of Peter and John, and perceived that they were unlearned and ignorant men, they marveled; and took knowledge of them, that they had been with Jesus* (Acts 4:13).

Renewal of Our Strength

Background Scripture: Isaiah 40:25-31

***But they that wait upon the Lord shall renew their strength; they shall mount up with wings as eagles; they shall run, and not be weary; and they shall walk, and not faint* (Isaiah 40:31).**

The late Commissioner Samuel Logan Brengle, D.D., D.F., of the Salvation Army writes, "If I were dying, and had the privilege of delivering a last exhortation to all the Christians of the world, and that message had to be condensed into three words, I would say, 'Wait on God.'"[1]

Why have so many deserted the army of the Lord and joined the ranks of Esau, King Saul and others who gave up the good fight of faith for what they thought would be an easier way? If you were to ask a group of those who have turned from following the straight and narrow way the reasons for their backsliding, various excuses would be given. But the real reason is they did not wait on God.

God's word warns us of our danger of leaving this Highway of Holiness in giving us examples of those who failed to wait on God, and turned back into sin. At the same time we have many illustrations of those who waited on God and mounted up with wings as an eagle to ever new heights in the spiritual realm.

Esau sold his birthright for one morsel of meat. His decision is an illustration of those who trade permanent and lasting values for the transitory pleasures of time. His desire for food was legitimate, and would have been satisfied lawfully, but Esau would not wait for God's timing. The flesh cried out for indulgence at any cost, and Esau yielded saying, "*Behold, I am at the point to die: and what profit shall this birthright do to me?*" (Genesis 25:32b). Then in verse 34b we read, "*...thus Esau despised his birthright.*"

Sin always looks different after it has been committed. "*Bread of deceit is sweet to a man; but afterwards his mouth shall be filled with gravel*" (Proverbs 20:17). The writer to the Hebrews records, "*For ye know how that afterward, when he would have inherited the blessing, he was rejected*" (Hebrews 12:17a). This all took place, because of a man who failed to wait and get his signals from God.

But Joseph is a model for all to follow in his example of waiting on God's timing. He was a young man far away from home in a foreign country. When he was seduced by Potiphar's wife he would not yield saying, "*...how then can I do this great wickedness, and sin against God*?" (Genesis 39:9b).

Although others are hurt when one sins, yet, Joseph realized that all sin is ultimately against God. This fact held Joseph steady in a time of what may have been a severe temptation. His decision not to yield caused him to bring down the wrath of Potiphar on him and a prison sentence. But, because Joseph waited on God all was working for his advancement and finally it put him in a position of influence where he was able to save his family from the destruction of famine, and was a link in the redemptive purpose of God for our salvation.

However fierce the temptation and battle, victory is certain if we wait on God and our trust is fully in Him.

Sing unto the Lord
(Psalm 30:4a)

"Waiting on the Lord, longing to mount higher;
Waiting on the Lord, having great desire;
Waiting on the Lord for the heavenly fire;
Waiting in the upper room."[2]

Verse to Memorize: *Wait on the Lord: be of good courage, and He shall strengthen thine heart: wait, I say, on the Lord* (Psalm 27:14).

The God We Serve

Background Scripture: Jeremiah 29:34

For I know the thoughts that I think toward you, saith the Lord, thoughts of peace and not of evil, to give you an expected end. Then shall ye call upon me, and ye shall go and pray unto me, and I will hearken unto you. And ye shall seek me, and find me, when ye shall search for me with all your heart **Jeremiah 29:11-13.**

What is our conception of God? The conclusion we reach will make the difference as to whether we become positive or negative Christians.

There are two extremes we must guard against. One to avoid, is viewing God as a doting, indulgent grandfather overlooking man's sin regarding such as mere human weakness of the flesh. God's norm for His people is that their hearts be cleansed from all sin by the fiery baptism of the Holy Spirit as it happened on the day of Pentecost. Yet many professed Christians are willing to settle for an experience that would permit one to sin in thought, word and deed everyday. God's word teaches there is a deeper spiritual experience for us.

The other extreme that we must shun is to think of God as so severe, unbending and ready to pronounce judgment for the least deviation from His perfection, that we no longer see God as our Father as described in Psalm 103:13-14, "*Like as a father pitieth his children, so the Lord pitieth them that fear Him. For He knoweth our frame; He remembereth that we are dust.*"

If we must call every mistake of judgment and such as sin, then no one would be able to live the sanctified life. Although we need to pray to God for forgiveness of our mistakes and blunders, trusting the precious blood of Jesus Christ to cover, yet only presumptuous sin will cause a break in our relationship with God.

Even if one should be so unfortunate as to fall into sin, he should not utterly despair, but immediately cling close to our Advocate (helper or attorney), remembering the word of God as found in I John 2:1-2, "*My little children, these things write I unto you, that ye sin not. And if any man sin, we have an Advocate with the Father, Jesus*

Christ the righteous: And He is the propitiation for our sins: And not for ours only, but also for the sins of the whole world."

This scripture in Jeremiah depicts God's people in a foreign land with many of them longing to return to their native land. It appears that they had a wrong conception of God, and by inference it appears they thought even God had turned against them.

If Satan can discourage us by such thoughts, then we do not have courage and faith to approach God. This is what happens when the enemy tricks a conscientious person into thinking he or she has committed an unpardonable sin. Such a person may despair, and give up the faith, but God never turns any away who sincerely desire Him and are hungering and thirsting after righteousness. There is such a sin for Jesus mentions it, but any that have committed this sin are no longer thirsting and hungering for God.

What does God say to these Jews in exile? "*For I know the thoughts that I think toward you, saith the Lord, thoughts of peace, and not of evil, to give you an expected end*" (Jeremiah 29:11). God is saying the same to us today.

Sing unto the Lord
(Psalm 30:4a)

What a Friend we have in Jesus, All our sins and griefs to bear!
What a privilege to carry Everything to God in prayer!
Oh, what peace we often forfeit, Oh, what needless pain we bear
All because we do not carry Everything to God in prayer![1]

Verse to Memorize: *It is good that a man should both hope and quietly wait for the salvation of the Lord* (Lamentations 3:26).

The Danger of Apathy

Background Scripture: Lamentations 1:1-12

***Is it nothing to you, all ye that pass by? behold, and see if there be any sorrow like unto my sorrow* (Lamentations 1:12a).**

Conditions in Judah had deteriorated. The Babylonian army under Nebuchadnezzar fought against Jerusalem for eighteen months. Although warned by Jeremiah the prophet to surrender, King Zedekiah refused to listen to God's message through the prophet, and the nation was conquered, and Judah experienced extreme suffering. The influential people were carried away to Babylon, and the poorest were left to be tillers of the soil.

This suffering of Judah was due to their rebellion and sin against God. In chapter 3:4a we read, "*We have transgressed and have rebelled.*" If not pardoned, sooner or later, sin is punished; Judah found this out to their sorrow.

God pleads with men to turn from sin and live. God spoke to Israel and said, "*...As I live, saith the Lord God, I have no pleasure in the death of the wicked; but that the wicked turn from his way and live: turn ye, turn ye from your evil ways; for why will ye die, O house of Israel?*" (Ezekiel 33:11b) Judah failed to heed the voice of God and suffered the consequences of their choice.

To add to their sorrow, those who took Judah captive required of them a song. It is recorded in Psalm 137:3-4, "*For there they that carried us away captive required of us a song; and they that wasted us required of us mirth, saying, Sing us one of the songs of Zion. How shall we sing the Lord's song in a strange land?*"

These people found out what all backsliders experience: when one leaves God, the song departs. King David realized this truth as he prayed for forgiveness and cleansing in Psalm 51:12-13, "*Restore unto me the joy of Thy salvation; and uphold me with Thy free spirit. Then will I teach transgressors Thy ways; and sinners shall be converted unto thee.*"

Some of the people who were carried away captive were satisfied to remain in Babylon. There is hope for the fallen who desire to return, but God honors man's freedom of choice and will not force him to follow in the "Way of Life."

But God always has a remnant who still serve Him even in times of extreme persecution and suffering when many are indifferent. Jeremiah was one of the faithful. He cries out, "*For these things I weep*" (Lamentations 1:16a).

One can become calloused to the suffering of humanity, and have an attitude of indifference, because of the sorrows all about, which are so common that they no longer affect us. Apathy seems to have been the problem with many in Judah. Some seem to have surrendered to what they thought was the inevitable. Yet, God's plan was to restore them to their homeland after seventy years of captivity.

Jeremiah cries out of his heart, "*Is it nothing to you, all ye that pass by?*" (Lamentations 1:12a). There is one thing that will keep us from becoming calloused to a world lost in sin, and that is to cultivate our own personal spiritual experience, and live close to God. This will keep pastor and people from becoming professional in their service to God, and keep us from apathy.

Sing unto the Lord
(Psalm 30:4a)

Down in the human heart, Crushed by the Tempter,
Feelings lie buried that grace can restore.
Touched by a loving heart, Wakened by kindness,
Chords that are broken will vibrate once more.[1]

Verse to Memorize: *Behold, this was the iniquity of thy sister Sodom, pride, fullness of bread; and abundance of idleness was in her and in her daughters, neither did she strengthen the hand of the poor and needy* (Ezekiel 16:49).

A Spiritual Heart Transplant

Background Scripture: Ezekiel 36:16-38

***A new heart also I will give you, and a new spirit will I put within you: and I will take away the stony heart out of your flesh, and I will give you an heart of flesh. And I will put my spirit within you, and cause you to walk in my statutes, and ye shall keep my judgments, and do them* (Ezekiel 36:26-27).**

A common thought among mankind is that a man is a sinner because he commits acts of sin, but both the Old Testament and the New Testament unite in teaching the fact that man commits sinful acts because he is first a sinner at heart.

Jesus made this truth clear by teaching that, "…*those things which proceed out of the mouth come forth from the heart; and they defile the man. For out of the heart proceed evil thoughts, murders, adulteries, fornications, thefts, false witness, blasphemies*" (Matthew 15:18b-19). In Jeremiah 17:9, God's word proclaims, "*The heart is deceitful above all things, and desperately wicked: who can know it?*"

There must be a spiritual heart transplant performed by God himself in order that a man may be enabled to live inwardly and outwardly as Christ taught us to live in the Sermon on the Mount.

A sinner may be able to refrain from outward gross acts of sin; then he is accountable only to God, but for some sins, an individual must not only answer to God, but also to society. So it is good for the sinner, and all of us that we have laws to curb these sinful acts of men.

But one cannot completely control a sinful heart by mere resolutions. "*Can the Ethiopian change his skin, or the leopard his spots? then may ye also do good, that are accustomed to do evil*" (Jeremiah 13:23). But thanks be to God that what is impossible with men is still possible with God, for our Savior, in speaking of the difficulty of rich men entering the Kingdom of God says, "*With men this is impossible; but with God all things are possible*" (Matthew 19:26b). St. Paul found the answer to this dilemma as recorded in Romans 7:24-25a, "*O wretched man that I am! who shall deliver me from the body of this death? I thank God through Jesus Christ our Lord.*"

Neither is seclusion the answer to the sin problem, or the monks would have already found the answer. They found Satan tempted them even in the monastery. Any wise Christian will not place himself or herself in the way of temptation; but there are times when duty calls us where we cannot avoid temptation. What then? Christ's keeping power is available at such times. Jesus prayed, "*I pray not that Thou shouldest take them out of the world, but that Thou shouldest keep them from the evil*" (St. John 17:15).

Is there any heart too sinful for God to change? Even some of God's people may nearly despair in believing for the salvation of some hardened sinners, but not God.

In one sense it is not sin or how great a sin that leads a man to hell but his failure to come to Christ and be forgiven and cleansed from sin. Jeremiah cries out, *"Is there no balm in Gilead; is there no physician there? why then is not the health of the daughter of my people recovered?"* (Jeremiah 8:22)

When one is converted he may feel no need for a further work of grace, but in time he will find there remains that in the heart which, "*...is not subject to the law of God, neither indeed can be*" (Romans 8:7b). When this need is realized the justified Christian should immediately make a full unconditional surrender to God and receive the baptism of the Holy Spirit and fire.

Yes, God is still changing stony hearts to hearts of flesh. Amen!

Sing unto the Lord
(Psalm 30:4a)

Rock of Ages, cleft for me.
Let me hide myself in Thee.
Let the water and the flood,
From Thy wounded side which flowed,
Be of sin the double cure,
Save from wrath and make me pure.[1]

Verse to Memorize: *And I will give them a heart to know me, that I am the Lord: and they shall be my people, and I will be their God; for they shall return unto me with their whole heart* (Jeremiah 24:7).

NOT FOR SALE

Background Scripture: Daniel 3:1-30

***If it be so, our God whom we serve is able to deliver us from the burning fiery furnace, and He will deliver us out of thine hand, O king. But if not, be it known unto thee, O king, that we will not serve thy gods, nor worship the golden image which thou hast set up* (Daniel 3:17-18).**

In writing to young men, St. John says, "*...I have written unto you, young men, because ye are strong, and the word of God abideth in you, and ye have overcome the wicked one*" (I John 2:14b). These words could well have been spoken of Shadrach, Meshach, and Abednego.

Here we have three young God-fearing men far away from the influence and restraints of parents and family, yet strong in faith, serving God. No doubt they, like every good Jew, repeated the Shema several times a day as recorded in Deuteronomy 6:4. "*Hear, O Israel: The Lord our God is one Lord.*" This truth surely ruled out the worshipping of the "*golden image that Nebuchadnezzar the king hath set up*" (Daniel 3:7b).

There is a time in our Christian walk that we must be decisive. These young people loved God and had all the facts in order to make an intelligent decision, so when given a second chance to worship the idol they had no need of debating the issue, for their minds were made up that they would serve God, and Him alone, whatever the cost might be. This goes a long way in facing all temptation.

There were two things these young men made clear to the king: God was able to deliver them, but if not, they would not bow to the idol.

Shadrach, Meshach and Abednego refused to worship the golden image and were cast into the overheated furnace. The king was astonished as he looked into the furnace and said, "*Lo, I see four men loose, and walking in the midst of the fire, and they have no hurt; and the form of the fourth is like the Son of God*" (Daniel 3:25b).

It is better and safer to suffer, enduring all sorts of persecution, trials and tests, so long as the Son of God is there with us, than to know the devil's peace.

In the highway of holiness, we must learn to walk by faith, and not by sight. I am not sure these young people knew for sure they would be delivered as the soldiers marched them up to the fiery furnace. Their humanity may have been very evident as the flesh cried out for deliverance even as Jesus facing the cross prayed to His Father, "*O My Father, if it be possible, let this cup pass from me: Nevertheless not as I will, but as Thou wilt*" (Matthew 26:39b). God's people live according to His word. Feelings fluctuate, but God's word "*shall not pass away*" (Matthew 24:39b).

So by faith the mature Christian serves God whatever may be his lot, and continues to live right even when God may seem to be far off. I attended a tent meeting some years ago, and the testimony of a young lady made an indelible impression on me. She said, "God doesn't have to bless me in order for me to serve him." God honors such a faith, and eventually this kind of faith is rewarded with a blessing.

May we all have such a dedication to God and his kingdom that we will faithfully serve God regardless of the consequences.

Sing Unto The Lord
(Psalm 30:4a)

Yield not to temptation, For yielding is sin.
Each victory will help you, Some other battle to win.
Fight manfully onward. Dark passions subdue.
Look ever to Jesus; He'll carry you through.[1]

Verse to Memorize: *There hath no temptation taken you but such as is common to man: but God is faithful, who will not suffer you to be tempted above that ye are able; but will with the temptation also make a way to escape, that ye may be able to bear it* (I Corinthians 10:13).

Hope for the Backslider

Background Scripture: Hosea 14:1-9

***I will heal their backsliding, I will love them freely: for mine anger is turned away from him* (Hosea 14:4).**

The casualty rate among God's people is extremely high in the spiritual warfare in which we are engaged. In warfare among nations there will be casualties, but in God's army there need be no casualties, for God has made provision to keep those He has rescued from the power of Satan. Jesus prayed for all of us. In St. John 17:11b our Saviour prayed thus, "*...Holy Father, keep through Thine own name those whom Thou hast given me, that they may be one, as we are.*"

With such provision made for our safety and victory in this conflict, why do so many turn back from following the Lord? In our churches we receive new Christians by profession of faith; but at the same time many leave us through the back door as casualties to the enemy. This should not be!

No doubt many have failed to go deep enough, the seed having fallen on the rocks and beaten paths. Others have made a good start grounded in the faith, but have allowed the cares of this life to choke the word, and turned back to the old life in which our Saviour speaks in Matthew 13:22, "*He also that received seed among the thorns is he that heareth the word; and the care of this world, and the deceitfulness of riches, choke the word, and he becometh unfruitful.*"

The backslider is the most miserable of all men on the face of the earth. The sinner has never experienced what the backslider had once enjoyed. The one who has turned away from following God has already tasted and found "*...that the Lord is good...*" (Psalm 34:8)

Is there any hope for such? The Bible says so, both in the Old Testament and the New Testament. Jesus says, "*How think ye? if a man have an hundred sheep, and one of them be gone astray, doth he not leave the ninety and nine, and goeth into the mountains, and seeketh that which is gone astray?*" (Matthew 18:12) The story of the prodigal son, also, illustrates God's love for the backslider. Hosea's love for his wife Gomer, even though she was unfaithful, again points out God's concern and love for those who have strayed from Him.

Listen to Christ in speaking of a backslider's return, "*Likewise, I say unto you, there is joy in the presence of the angels of God over one sinner that repenteth*" (Luke 15:10).

Those of us who are still in the fold need to take the responsibility of helping to restore those who have fallen by the wayside. "*Brethern, if a man be overtaken in a fault, ye which are spiritual, restore such an one in the spirit of meekness; considering thyself, lest thou also be tempted*" (Galatians 6:1).

The backslider, after having failed, is already discouraged and perhaps wondering if there is any use of trying again. He needs someone of faith to stand by him and encourage him to see he can still make it. God's word says so, "*I will love them freely: for mine anger is turned away from him*" (Hosea 14:4).

Some backslider may ask, "Will I ever fly as high again?" Listen again to God's answer in speaking of the backslider, "*His branches shall spread, and his beauty shall be as the olive tree, and his smell as Lebanon*" (Hosea 14:16).

Backslider, you can be restored if you truly repent and trust in Christ with all your heart as Lord and Saviour. Satan will desperately try to keep you in his clutches, but there is victory, "*If God be for us, who can be against us?*" (Romans 8:31b) And I can assure you on the authority of God's word that our God is for us. I have found it so. "*...him that cometh to me I will in no wise cast out*" (St. John 6:37b). Praise be to God!

Sing Unto The Lord
(Psalm 30:4a)

The great Physician now is near,
The sympathizing Jesus.
He speaks the drooping heart to cheer.
Oh, hear the voice of Jesus.[1]

Verse to Memorize: *Turn, O backsliding children, saith the Lord; for I am married unto you: and I will take you one of a city, and two of a family, and I will bring you to Zion* (Jeremiah 3:14).

The Pentecost Yet to Come

Background Scripture: Joel 2:28-32

And it shall come to pass afterward, that I will pour out my Spirit upon all flesh; and your sons and your daughters shall prophesy, your old men shall dream dreams, your young men shall see visions: And also upon the servants and upon the handmaids in those days will I pour out my Spirit **(Joel 1:29).**

In his sermon at Pentecost, the Apostle Peter referred to this passage from the Book of Joel as being fulfilled in that, which had just taken place in the lives of the 120 who tarried in the upper room until they were filled with the Holy Spirit.

The Patriarchs and saints of old had the promise of a better day to come in the dispensation of God's grace and by faith laid hold on the promise. The Hebrew writer mentions this in Hebrews 11:39-40, where he writes, "*and these all, having obtained a good report through faith, received not the promise: God having provided some better thing for us, that they without us should not be made perfect.*"

The prophet Joel makes it clear that God makes no distinction in regard to fulfilling his promise to pour out His Spirit upon all flesh. Some may entertain the thought that this deeper experience of grace is for the leaders, and an elect few only, but the anointed prophet writes that all may claim the promise.

I know of a drunkard of whom many had despaired of his ever finding Christ as Saviour. But he prayed clear through and then was filled with the Holy Spirit and became a mighty power for God. Although in heaven now, the influence of his godly life remains an inspiration to me.

No distinctions are made as the writer to the Hebrews, in referring to this experience of grace, writes, "*Wherefore Jesus also, that He might sanctify the people with his own blood, suffered without the gate*" (Hebrews 13:12).

Not only does this experience purify our hearts by faith, but we are empowered by the Holy Spirit to proclaim the good news to a needy and dying world. There is work for all regardless of sex, age, bond or free, according to this scripture.

There are no discharges in the army of the Lord. Some older servants of God may feel they no longer have anything to contribute in the building of God's kingdom. But our scripture lets us know that old men will still have dreams when filled with the Holy Spirit.

Martin Luther King said, "I have a dream." Because of his untimely death, he did not see it fulfilled, but others picked up the cause and carried it on to fruition.

We who are advanced in years must not lose our zeal, but though not able to actively do as much work, we can see our dreams come to pass by encouraging younger people in their work for God by our prayers and doing what we are still able to do.

We are now living in the Holy Spirit Dispensation. The promise is now available. Let us proclaim this truth to the uttermost parts of this world.

Sing Unto The Lord
(Psalm 30:4a)

Have you ever felt the power of the Pentecostal fire,
Burning up all carnal nature, Cleansing out all base desire,
Going through and through your spirit, Cleansing all its stain away?
Oh, I'm glad, so glad to tell you It is for us all today.[1]

Verses to Memorize: *Then Peter said unto them, Repent, and be baptized every one of you in the name of Jesus Christ for the remission of sins, and ye shall receive the gift of the Holy Ghost. For the promise is unto you, and to your children, and to all that are afar off, even as many as the Lord our God shall call* (Acts 2:38-39).

A Famine for the Word of God

***Behold, the days come, saith the Lord God, that I will send a famine in the land, not a famine of bread, nor a thirst for water, but of hearing the words of the Lord; And they shall wander from sea to sea, and from the north even to the east, they shall run to and fro to seek the word of the Lord, and shall not find it* (Amos 8:11-12).**

Ordinarily when we think of famine we associate it with the scarcity of food, but in this scripture there is a famine revealed that has far sorer consequences than a famine of hunger for the bread that sustains a man's physical life. We are not minimizing the suffering that accompanies the famine of bread, as we read in Lamentations 4:9, "*They that be slain with the sword are better than they that be slain with hunger: for these pine away, stricken through for want of the fruits of the field.*"

But we reiterate there is a famine that is much worse than a famine of bread, for our Saviour says, "*...Man shall not live by bread alone, but by every word that proceedeth out of the mouth of God*" (Matthew 4:4b). A man may die of starvation, yet, live if he has been a partaker of the Bread of Life. Jesus says, "*I am the living Bread which came down from heaven: If any man eat of this Bread, he shall live forever: and the Bread that I will give is my flesh, which I will give for the life of the world*" (St. John 6:51).

The prophet Amos foresees a day coming when those who rejected the message of the prophets will hunger to hear a message preached from the Word of God.

Do we have the longing for the Word of God as the Psalmist had when he said, "*O how love I Thy law! It is my meditation all the day*" (Psalm 119:97). Those of us who have free access to God's word may find it difficult to realize what a famine of God's message would really be.

I fear we often take the Church and the Word of God for granted and fail to realize the loss we would sustain if we were denied our freedom of worship. The ark of the Lord which symbolized the presence of God to Israel was taken captive by the Philistines and when returned we read, "*...and they lifted up their eyes, and saw the ark, and rejoiced to see it" (I Samuel 6:13b).* Let us rejoice we have "*The sincere milk of the word, that ye may grow thereby*" (I Peter 2:2b).

We need to memorize the Word of God, for the time could come when we would be denied free access to God's Word. The Psalmist said, "*Thy word have I hid in my heart, that I might not sin against Thee*" (Psalm 119:11).

May the Holy Spirit so inspire us as we read the written Word, that we may be lead to the Living Word, our Lord Jesus Christ, who came to give life to this world.

Sing Unto The Lord
(Psalm 30:4a)

Break thou the bread of life, Dear Lord to me,
As Thou didst break the loaves Beside the sea.
Beyond the sacred page I seek Thee, Lord
My spirit pants for Thee, O living word![1]

Verse to Memorize: *Heaven and earth shall pass away, but my words shall not pass away (*Matthew 24:35).

The Way Up is Down

***The pride of thine heart hath deceived thee, thou that dwellest in the clefts of the rock, whose habitation is high; that saith in his heart, who shall bring me down to the ground? Though thou exalt thyself as the eagle, and though thou set thy nest among the stars, thence will I bring thee down, saith the Lord* (Obadiah 3-4).**

There are laws in the spiritual realm which are as certain and dependable as the law of gravity is in the physical realm or material domain. In either, these laws cannot be violated without suffering severe consequences. Jesus says, "*And whosoever shall fall on this stone shall be broken: but on whomsoever it shall fall, it will grind him to powder*" (Matthew 21:44).

The great sin of Edom was pride from which all their other sins sprang. They failed to trust in God for their security, but trusted in the natural fortress, high in the clefts of the rock, a position which was practically inaccessible. For many generations the Edomites had lived in seemingly security. No enemy had been able to penetrate or enter the narrow canyon which led to their chief cities that were hewn out of the rocky mountain walls,[1] but when an individual or nation sins against God by trusting in their own strength, and in their pride, and no longer relies on God, then eventually they fall. Listen to what God says, "*A man's pride shall bring him low: but honour shall uphold the humble in spirit*" (Proverbs 29:23).

Here is a warning for America. We cannot trust in our strength as a super power for our security. The Psalmist observed that, "*An horse is a vain thing for safety: neither shall he deliver any by his great strength*" (Psalm 33:17). When a nation rejects God, and fails to repent it is only a matter of time until that kingdom falls.

King Nebuchadnezzar illustrates this truth. The account is given in Daniel 4:29-31. "*At the end of twelve months he walked in the palace of the kingdom of Babylon. The king spake, and said, Is not this great Babylon that I have built for the house of the kingdom by the might of my power, and for the honour of my majesty? While the word was in the king's mouth, there fell a voice from heaven, saying, O king Nebuchadnezzar to thee it is spoken; The kingdom is departed from thee.*"

God is no respecter of persons. The only alternative in order to prevent judgment on a sinful nation or individual is found in II Chronicles 7:14. "*If my people, which are called by my name, shall humble themselves, and pray, and seek my face, and turn from their wicked ways; then will I hear from heaven, and will forgive their sin, and will heal their land.*"

Sing unto the Lord
(Psalm 30:4a)

Sinners Jesus will receive;
Sound the word of grace to all
Who the heavenly pathway leave,
All who linger, all who fall.[2]

Verse to Memorize: *And whosoever shall exalt himself shall be abased; and he that shall humble himself shall be exalted* (Matthew 23:12).

GENUINE REPENTANCE

And Jonah began to enter into the city a day's journey, and he cried, and said, yet forty days, and Nineveh shall be overthrown. So the people of Nineveh believed God, and proclaimed a fast, and put on sackcloth, from the greatest of them even to the least of them. For word came unto the king of Nineveh, and he arose from his throne, and he laid his robe from him, and covered him with sackcloth, and sat in ashes. And he caused it to be proclaimed and published through Nineveh by the decree of the king and his nobles, saying, Let neither man nor beast, herd or flock, taste anything: let them not feed, nor drink water: But let man and beast be covered with sackcloth, and cry mightily unto God: yea, let them turn everyone from his evil way, and from the violence that is in their hands. Who can tell if God will turn and repent, and turn away from His fierce anger, that we perish not? And God saw their works, that they turned from their evil way; and God repented of the evil, that He had said that He would do unto them; and He did it not **(Jonah 3:4-10).**

In this passage of Scripture we have an illustration of God's willingness to forgive when sinful man meets the conditions set forth by God for genuine repentance.

Jonah could only see Nineveh as a wicked heathen city to be destroyed, but God who "*is longsuffering to us-ward, not willing that any should perish, but that all should come to repentance*" (II Peter 3:9b) saw this city as the object of His compassion. God always looks beyond the marred vessel and sees the potential of sinful man when placed in the hands of the Master Potter. Where would we all be if it were not for the mercy and love of our caring Lord?

With very little instruction, if any, this heathen king led his people to genuine repentance. God's word reveals the fact that enough light is given to every son and daughter of Adam's race to bring them to "*the true Light, which lighteth every man that cometh into the world*" (St. John 1:9b).

God looks on the intent of the heart as we pray rather than the words we say, and the Holy Spirit who "*maketh intercession for us with groanings which cannot be uttered*" (Romans 8:26b) will also intercede for the sinner who draws nigh to God in genuine repentance.

Much of the repentance of the king and the people of Nineveh consisted of them humbling themselves before God with fasting and covering their bodies with sackcloth, and sitting in ashes. In verse 10 we read, "*And God saw their works, that they turned from their evil way; and God repented of the evil, that he said that he would do unto them; and He did it not.*"

One of the sad events in the history of our country was the betrayal of the nation by Julius and Ethel Rosenburg during the administration of President Dwight D. Eisenhower. This couple was convicted of treason and sentenced to death for their crime. What made it even sadder was the fact that their lives would be spared if they only confessed and met the requirements set forth by the court. After all these intervening years, I still remember our President standing by until the last, ready to save their lives, but Julius and Ethel Rosenburg refused the pardon and were executed.

Oh, how many are lost in an everlasting hell because they refused to accept the pardon purchased through the blood of our blessed Lord and Saviour Jesus Christ. Be wise and enter the fold while the door is still open. Heed God's word as found in Hebrews 3:15b, "*Today if ye will hear His voice, harden not your hearts, as in the provocation.*"

Sing unto the Lord
(Psalm 30:4a)

Ye who are troubled and burdened by sin,
Come just as you are.
Come to the Saviour, a new life begin.
Oh, come just as you are![2]

Verse to Memorize: *Seek ye the Lord while He may be found, call ye upon Him while He is near: Let the wicked forsake his way, and the unrighteous man his thoughts: and let him return unto the Lord, and He will have mercy upon him; and to our God, for He will abundantly pardon* (Isaiah 55:6-7).

God's Requirements

Wherewith shall I come before the Lord, and bow myself before the high God? shall I come before Him with burnt offerings, with calves of a year old? Will the Lord be pleased with thousands of rams, or with ten thousands of rivers of oil? shall I give my first born for my transgression, the fruit of my body for the sin of my soul? He hath shewed thee, O man, what is good; and what doth the Lord require of thee, but to do justly, and to love mercy, and to walk humbly with thy God? (Micah 6:6-8)

The Gospel is not complex and complicated. St. Paul in writing to the Corinthians states, "*But I fear, lest by any means, as the serpent beguiled Eve through his subtlety, so your minds should be corrupted from the simplicity that is in Christ*" (II Corinthians 11:3). On this verse, John Wesley comments, "That simplicity which is lovingly intent on Him alone, seeking no other person or thing."[1]

When a lawyer asked the Master which is the great commandment in the law; Jesus condensed the entire law as consisting of our love to God and our neighbor. When the early church came together to consider what was necessary for the Gentiles to observe in order to follow Christ, they came to the consensus as found in Acts 15:28-29 where we read, "*For it seemed good to the Holy Ghost, and to us to lay upon you no greater burden than these necessary things; That ye abstain from meats offered to idols, and from blood, and from things strangled, and from fornication: from which if ye keep yourselves, ye shall do well. Fare ye well.*"

If it were necessary for us to meet the requirements laid by men in order to serve Christ, none would meet such demands. Jesus realized this truth as He spoke of the Scribes and the Pharisees, saying, "*For they bind heavy burdens and grievous to be borne, and lay them on men's shoulders; but they themselves will not move them with one of their fingers*" (Matthew 23:4). How unlike the meek and lowly Jesus who speaks of His yoke as easy and His burden as being light.

Of all the courses of study offered by a school in order for a student to graduate, some are required while others are elective. Even so, God has some requirements if we are to be His genuine followers, which are: to do justly, to love mercy and to walk humbly with God.

In order to meet these requirements our hearts must be changed by the new birth, and then cleansed by the fiery baptism of the Holy Spirit.

Sing unto the Lord (Psalm 30:4a)

His yoke is easy; His burden is light.
I've found it so; I've found it so.
He leadeth me by day and by night
Where living waters flow.[2]

Verse to Memorize: *Come unto Me, all ye that labor and are heavy laden, and I will give you rest* (Matthew 11:28).

A Secure Fortress

***The Lord is good, a stronghold in the day of trouble; and He knoweth them that trust in Him* (Nahum 1:7).**

God extends his goodness to those who hate Him and refuse the invitation to drink from the fountain of living waters. In speaking of His Father, Jesus says, "*...He maketh His sun to rise on the evil and on the good, and sendeth rain on the just and on the unjust*" (Matthew 5:45b).

But one will never realize how great and good our God is until he experiences an intimate relationship with Him. St. Paul writes of this close relationship between God and His children in I Corinthians 6:17, "*But he that is joined unto the Lord is one spirit.*" One must first become a son or daughter of God in order to understand or fully appreciate this truth. King David doesn't argue with those outside of God's Kingdom in order to convince the wayward of the goodness of God, but cries out to all who will hear, "*O taste and see that the Lord is good: blessed is the man that trusteth in Him*" (Psalm 34:8).

God is not only good, but He is a stronghold in the day of trouble. In the book of Job, Eliphaz the Temanite observed the safety of those who put their trust in God. He says, "*He shall deliver thee in six troubles: yea, in seven there shall no evil touch thee*" (Job 5:19).

I have often wondered how people live or can face life rejecting the true and only source of their security both for this life and for the life to come. As with Joshua, I can testify after suffering many difficult experiences during a long lifetime, that not one of God's promises has failed. His promise to safely lead me through the valley of the shadow of death, and give me a safe landing on that beautiful shore will be kept in like manner. Why not end your search for security by coming to God, and finding what the Hebrew writer speaks of "*...as an anchor of the soul, both sure and stedfast...*" (Hebrews 6:19)

Then we see the delight God takes in those who genuinely trust in Him. We must trust our heavenly Father even as children trust their earthly parents. I grew up during the great depression, but never once did I worry about something to eat, for I trusted my parents. Jesus says, "*Verily I say unto you, Except ye be converted, and become as little children, ye shall not enter into the kingdom of heaven*" (Matthew 18:3b).

During a storm I watched a bird perched on a tender branch outside the window. The fierce wind blew that bush, but the little bird held on as though in prayer, quietly trusting its Heavenly Father who in speaking of sparrows says, "*Are not two sparrows sold for a farthing? and one of them shall not fall on the ground without your Father*" (Matthew 10:29). This incident served as a faith tonic for me to trust my Heavenly Father when sailing through the difficult storms of life.

Sing Unto The Lord
(Psalm 30:4a)

A mighty Fortress is our God,
A Bulwark never failing;
Our helper He, amid the flood
of mortal ills prevailing.[1]

Verse to Memorize: *Or despisest thou the riches of His goodness and forbearance and longsuffering; not knowing that the goodness of God leadeth thee to repentance?* (Romans 2:4)

A Faith that will not Shrink

***Although the fig tree shall not blossom; neither shall fruit be in the vines; the labour of the olive shall fail, and the fields shall yield no meat; the flock shall be cut off from the fold, and there shall be no herd in the stalls; Yet I will rejoice in the Lord, I will joy in the God of my salvation. The Lord God is my strength, and He will make my feet like hind's feet, and He will make me to walk upon mine high places* (Habakkuk 3:17-19a).**

Why are some people able to be content and rejoice in the Lord, though they have very little of the material wealth of this world, while others who are blessed with the material wealth of this present age are discontented and unhappy? As we study God's Word, and observe mankind in everyday practical living, we are forced to conclude that genuine peace, happiness, and a sense of well-being is not contingent upon our circumstances.

The prophet, Habukkuk, had many things that tried and tested his faith, but finally he stopped his attempt to reason out the providential dealings of God with man, and declares, "*But the just shall live by his faith*" (Habukkuk 2:4b). He sees there are some things in this life we experience that we will never understand until we enter those pearly gates. Then when we see Jesus we will not even think of asking about the things that are seemingly mysteries in this life. St. Paul writes, "*For now we see through a glass darkly; but then face to face: now I know in part; but then shall I know even as also I am known*" (I Corinthians 13:12).

The prophet portrays a very black and desolate picture in verse 17 of what could happen to him, but like St. Paul in Romans 8:37, declares, "*Yet I will rejoice in the Lord, I will joy in the God of my salvation*" (Verse 18).

Only the man or woman fully and unconditionally surrendered to God can proclaim such a statement as found in verse 18. There are times when there seems to be no way over, under, or around a problem, yet, God makes a way.

Habukkuk concludes his testimony by saying, God "*will make my feet like hinds' feet*" (In verse 19). Did you ever notice how gracefully a deer clears an obstacle? When we put our confidence and faith in God, He will do the same for us.

Sing unto the Lord
(Psalm 30:4a)

No matter what may be the test,
God will take care of you.
Lean, weary one, upon His breast;
God will take care of you.[1]

Verse to Memorize: ...*For I know whom I have believed, and am persuaded that He is able to keep that which I have committed unto Him against that day* (II Timothy 1:12b).

Zephaniah

A Time to Rejoice

***Sing, O daughter of Zion; shout, O Israel; be glad and rejoice with the heart, O daughter of Jerusalem* (Zephaniah 3:14).**

In a time of universal corruption, God still had a remnant in Israel who was loyal to God and His cause. Not only was the cup of iniquity full in the heathen nations, but sin was rampant even in Jerusalem as we read, "*And it shall come to pass at that time, that I will search Jerusalem with candles, and punish the men that are on their lees: that say in their heart, The Lord will not do good, neither will He do evil*" (Zephaniah 1:12).

Yet God always will have a remnant that love and serve Him. Why could these people rejoice and sing while nations including Israel, were threatened with judgment? It was because they had fled to their city of refuge, and gained their freedom through faith in the death and resurrection of their Great High Priest.

Evangelist Rev. E. J. Hundley testified as to how he had settled out of court. That is why these people could be joyful for they, too, settled the sin issue out of court as recorded in chapter 3:15, "*The Lord hath taken away thy judgments, He hath cast out thine enemy: the king of Israel, even the Lord, is in the midst of thee: thou shalt not see evil any more.*"

Years ago, I heard a lady ask the question, "How can people shout when there is so much sorrow in the world?" I can sympathize with her concern for the suffering we see about us, but the only satisfactory answer is Jesus Christ our Lord and Saviour, who enables us to follow in His footsteps, "*Looking unto Jesus the author and finisher of our faith; who for the joy that was set before Him endured the cross, despising the shame, and is set down at the right hand of the throne of God*" (Hebrews 12:2). Jesus wants all of His followers to rejoice with Him even in the deepest of sorrows. As Jesus came near the time of His suffering in the garden, and later on the cross, He spoke to His disciples, saying, "*These things have I spoken unto you, that my joy might remain in you, and that your joy might be full*" (St. John 5:11).

I have not seen people drawn to God by a sad countenance, but I have noticed how sinners respond to the call of God when the Holy Spirit comes upon a service, and people are rejoicing in our God for all His love to us. Even before Jesus appeared, men and women came to God when they saw God revealed in the life and experience of His people. King Asa led his people in a revival that not only revived his own people, but spread to other tribes when they saw God was in it.

The Scripture says that Asa "*...gathered all Judah and Benjamin, and the strangers with them out of Ephraim and Manasseh, and out of Simeon: for they fell to him out of Israel in abundance, when they saw that the Lord his God was with him*" (II Chronicles 15:9b).

Sing unto the Lord
(Psalm 30:4a)

O happy day that fixed my choice
on Thee, my Saviour and my God!
Well may this glowing heart rejoice,
And tell its raptures all abroad.[1]

Verse to Memorize: *Then he said unto them, Go your way, eat the fat, and drink the sweet, and send portions unto them for whom nothing is prepared: for this day is holy unto our Lord: neither be ye sorry; for the joy of the Lord is your strength* (Nehemiah 8:10).

The Danger of Procrastination

Background Scripture: Haggai 1, 2

***Thus speaketh the Lord of hosts, saying, This people say, The time is not come, the time that the Lord's house should be built* (Haggai 1:2).**

Our blessed Lord and Saviour, Jesus Christ, the "Ancient of Days" who had never been bound by the limitations of time in His incarnation, and "*made like unto His brethren*" (Hebrews 2:17 partial), was keenly aware of the value of time. In St. John 9:4, the Master said, "*I must work the works of Him that sent me, while it is day: the night cometh, when no man can work.*"

Jesus was never too early or too late. There were times when men thought the Saviour failed to be on time as in the sickness and death of Lazarus, but Jesus always has a purpose and reason for His seeming delays in answering our urgent prayers. Lazarus died as we read in St. John 11:14-15b, "*Then said Jesus unto them plainly, Lazarus is dead. And I am glad for your sakes that I was not there, to the intent ye may believe.*"

The people in the time of Haggai realized that the house of the Lord should be built, but said this was not the time to build. Right at this point is Satan's strategy to rob and defeat us. If we wait until everything is in perfect order to do God's will, we will never accomplish God's purpose in our lives. "*The slothful man saith, There is a lion without, I shall be slain in the streets*" (Proverbs 22:13). But as John Bunyan observed the lions were all chained. God's Word in Ecclesiastes 11:4 says, "*He that observeth the wind shall not sow; and he that regardeth the clouds shall not reap.*"

Procrastination is deadly in all areas of our living on earth where time is so fleeting. The present moment is so fleeting that we can hardly measure the present. So we live mostly with the past or future in view. God's plan is for us to grasp the present moment and do what pleases Him moment by moment.

One of Satan's greatest weapons in destroying souls is when he suggests that one should repent and accept Christ, but the time is not now.

The illustration is given of a minister who was planning to preach the text, "*Behold, now is the accepted time; behold, now is the day of salvation.*" While in his study meditating upon the subject he fell asleep and dreamed that he saw Satan and the fallen angels gathered for the purpose of devising ways and means by which they might effectively damn souls. He said that in the dreams he saw an infernal spirit arise and say, "I will go and tell the people there is no God." But Satan said, "That will not do, for only fools deny that fact."

Then another fiend, of unusual intelligence, arose and said, "I will go and tell them that there is nothing to religion; that it is all a farce."

But Satan replied, "That will never do, for multitudes have seen saints die, in sight of heaven, declaring that salvation was real."

One after another arose making suggestions, but Satan refused them all. Finally the subtlest of all arose and said, "I will go and tell them that there is a God; that the Bible is true; that salvation is real, but that there is plenty of time."

The minister said that in the dream he could see all were jubilant and Satan said, "Go! that is the plan." And the meeting disbanded.[1]

Sing unto the Lord
(Psalm 30:4a)

"Almost persuaded" now to believe;
"Almost persuaded" Christ to receive;
Seems now some soul to say, "Go, Spirit, go Thy way,
Some more convenient day on Thee I'll call."[2]

Verse to Memorize: ...*Today if ye will hear His voice, harden not your hearts, as in the provocation* (Hebrews 3:15b).

A Sure Cure for Sin

Background Scripture: Zechariah 12-13:1

***In that day there shall be a fountain opened to the house of David and to the inhabitants of Jerusalem for sin and for uncleanness* (Zechariah 13:1).**

Zechariah writing under Divine inspiration foresaw the day when the perfect Sacrifice for sin would be ushered in with a fountain opened "*for sin and uncleanness.*" In Hebrews 7:19 we read, "*For the law made nothing perfect, but the bringing in of a better hope did; by which we draw nigh unto God.*"

The Jews will eventually acknowledge that they crucified their Messiah, and accept Jesus Christ as the Lord and Saviour. We read the account in chapter 12 and verse 10, "*And I will pour upon the house of David, and upon the inhabitants of Jerusalem, the spirit of grace and of supplication: and they shall look upon me whom they have pierced, and they shall mourn for him, as one mourneth for his only son, and shall be in bitterness for him, as one that is in bitterness for his firstborn.*" The Jews will then be brought into the Christian Church.

Today this fountain for sin and uncleanness is open wide for both the Jew and Gentile. No matter how deep the stain of sin has gone, none need panic of despair, for no soul has ever been lost or turned away who has genuinely repented and accepted the "*Lamb of God, which taketh away the sin of the world*" (St. John 1:29b).

The unbelief of the Jews barred them from partaking of the benefits of Christ's atonement, and this same "*stumbling block*" will prevent Gentiles as well from entering the fold.

If the awakened Jews will mourn, as recorded in chapter 12:11-14, even though repentance has been granted; what will the anguish and remorse be of those who refuse Christ and "*make their bed in hell*" for all of eternity?

It is the part of wisdom to accept Christ here and now, not just in order to escape hell, but to know the best and fullest life possible on earth by becoming a friend of Jesus. "*...godliness is profitable unto* *all things, having promise of the life that now is, and of that which is to come*" (I Timothy 4:8b). If you are hungry and thirsty for that which will satisfy, come and plunge into the fountain and be made whole.

Sing Unto The Lord
(Psalm 30:4a)

Come Thou Fount of every blessing,
Tune my heart to sing Thy grace.
Streams of mercy, never ceasing,
Call for songs of loudest praise.
Teach me some melodious sonnet,
Sung by flaming tongues above.
Praise the Mount! I'm fixed upon it,
Mount of God's unchanging love.[1]

Verse to Memorize: *And she shall bring forth a Son, and thou shalt call His name Jesus: for He shall save His people from their sins* (Matthew 1:21).

The Windows of Heaven Opened

Background Scripture: Malachi 1:6-14; 3:4-12

***Bring ye all the tithes into the storehouse, that there may be meat in mine house, and prove me now herewith, saith the Lord of hosts, if I will not open you the windows of heaven, and pour you out a blessing, that there shall not be room enough to receive it* (Malachi 3:10).**

Many of the Jews, who had returned from exile, were disillusioned, because their high hopes were not yet fulfilled. They had been so long dominated by foreign nations that many had lost faith in their unique election of God to be a chosen people who would be a blessing to all the nations through the coming of the Messiah.

Because of their lack of faith and discouragement, many had ceased to live separated lives, and had absorbed the practices of their pagan neighbors. Yet, in the darkest days of moral corruption, God has always had those who love and fear Him. It was so in the time of Malachi as found in 3:16: "*Then they that feared the Lord spake often one to another: and the Lord hearkened, and heard it, and a book of remembrance was written before Him for them that feared the Lord, and that thought upon His name.*"

In calling this people to return to God, Malachi mentions various spiritual needs, but a dominant note that is repeated is their failure as being stewards of that with which God entrusted them. The law required that their sacrifice be perfect; but they evidently were offering blind and lame animals (1:8). Malachi says to offer the sacrifice to the governor and asks the people if their governor would be pleased or accept it. Of course, the answer would be *no.*

This scripture plainly teaches us if we want the windows of heaven opened on our thirsty souls, there must be an unconditional surrender to God without any reservation. In the closing days of World War II, after having dropped two atomic bombs on Japan, our country demanded unconditional surrender of the enemy. Japan was reluctant and fearful of the consequences, but after a full surrender they found the United States helpful in supplying food, and perhaps other needs.

It is the same when we surrender unconditionally to God. We find God blesses us in a way that we would have thought impossible. Listen to God's Word, "*But as it is written, Eye hath not seen, nor ear heard, neither have entered into the heart of man, the things which God hath prepared for them that love Him*" (I Corinthians 2:9).

The God-fearing man or woman not only gladly tithes but also goes beyond the letter of the law and realizes God owns all, and that they are His stewards. "...*God loveth a cheerful giver*" (II Corinthians 9:7b). Tithing was practiced long before the law was given, for we find Abram giving tithes to God through Melchizedek (Genesis 14:20). Jesus teaches we should tithe as found in Matthew 23:23.

Tithing is still God's plan for financing His Church. Personally, in my pastorates, I have never resorted to the practice of buying and selling in the name of the church in order to raise money for Kingdom needs. As a result I have found the needs amply met when people honor God by supporting His church with His plan of meeting the needs.

Also I can testify as to God's faithfulness as we practiced our personal stewardship. During a lengthy illness, while dependent on relatives for support, our regular income was two dollars per week, but God received twenty cents of that amount and God was faithful in making a way. Bless his Name!

Sing Unto The Lord
(Psalm 30:4a)

My Father is rich in houses and lands;
He holdeth the wealth of the world in His hands!
Of rubies and diamonds, of silver and gold,
His coffers are full-He has riches untold.[1]

Verse to Memorize: *And God is able to make all grace abound toward you; that ye, always having all sufficiency in all things, may abound to every good work: (As it is written, He hath dispersed abroad; he hath given to the poor: his righteousness remaineth forever* (II Corinthians 9:8-9).

Building for Eternity

***Therefore whosoever heareth these sayings of mine, and doeth them, I will liken him unto a wise man, which built his house upon a rock: And the rain descended, and the floods came, and the winds blew, and beat upon that house; and it fell not: for it was founded upon a rock. And everyone that heareth these sayings of mine, and doeth them not, shall be likened unto a foolish man, which built his house upon the sand: And the rain descended, and the floods came, and the winds blew, and beat upon that house; and it fell: and great was the fall of it* (St. Matthew 7:24-27).**

Our eternal destiny depends on the choices we make during our probation on earth; whether we build on the sinking sands of time or on Christ the Solid Rock.

As we see in this scripture, the identical storms will beat upon the house built on the Rock the same as that house built on the sand. As Christians, we are not immune from the common and everyday problems that confront all men. If Christians were immune, many would accept Christ as insurance against such suffering, even as the people who were miraculously fed by our Saviour sought after Jesus the next day with their ulterior motives. Listen to our Lord's insight. "*Jesus answered them and said, Verily, verily I say unto you, ye seek me, not because ye saw the miracles, but because ye did eat of the loaves, and were filled*" (St. John 6:26). God looks for people like Job, who in the midst of suffering, cried out, "*Though He slay me, yet will I trust in Him…*" (Job 13:15a)

What advantage then has a follower of Christ over those who reject Him? Even as Jesus was on board when the disciples were in jeopardy on the storm tossed boat on the Sea of Galilee, in a special way, God is with His Servants in the storms of life and will enable us to face the judgment washed clean in the precious blood of Christ which was shed for our redemption.

Adam Clark, in his comment on this passage, writes, "There are three general kinds of trials to which the followers of God are exposed, and to which some think, our Lord alludes here. First, those of temporal afflictions, coming in the course of Divine providence; these may be likened to the torrents of rain; second, those which come from the passions of men, and which may be likened to the impetuous rivers; third, those which come from Satan and his angels, and which, like tempestuous whirlwinds, threaten to carry everything before them. He alone whose soul is built on the Rock of Ages stands all the shocks; and not only stands in, but profits by them."[1]

Yes, we are building for eternity. As a teenager, I built a chicken house, which required very little foundation. In later years, I visited the Union Terminal Tower in Cleveland, Ohio. I read from a brochure how in the construction of that building the workers dug deep and laid the foundation on rock. What makes the difference? A chicken house is not expected to last long, and represents the temporal, while the Terminal Tower illustrates the eternal.

When God created man in His own image (Genesis 1:26) it meant that man was destined to live forever. Let us choose wisely and build on Christ the Solid Rock. "*...I have set before you life and death, blessing and cursing: therefore choose life, that both thou and thy seed may live*" (Deuteronomy 30:19 part).

Sing unto the Lord
(Psalm 30:4a)

My hope is built on nothing less
Than Jesus' blood and righteousness.
I dare not trust the sweetest frame,
But wholly lean of Jesus' name.
On Christ the solid Rock, I stand;
all other ground is sinking sand.[2]

Verse to Memorize: *For other foundation can no man lay than that is laid, which is Jesus Christ (I Corinthians* 3:11).

The Proof of Our Love

Background Scripture: St. Mark 5:1-20

And when He was come into the ship, he that had been possessed with the devil prayed Him that he might be with Him. Howbeit Jesus suffered him not, but saith unto him, Go home to thy friends, and tell them how great things the Lord hath done for thee, and hath had compassion on thee. And he departed, and began to publish in Decapolis how great things Jesus had done for him: and all man did marvel **(Mark 5:18-20).**

Jesus forgave a woman who had committed many sins, but came to the Master with a broken and contrite heart, displaying deep affection. The Saviour makes a very significant statement in St. Luke 7:47, "*Wherefore I say unto thee, her sins, which are many, are forgiven; for she loved much: but to whom little is forgiven; the same loveth little.*"

It was even so with the man with the unclean spirit in this scripture. He had been bound and enslaved in sin, a terror to all he came in contact with, but Jesus saved him and so changed this man who had been possessed with the devil, that he fell in love with his Master, and wanted to follow Jesus everywhere He went.

This reaction is the normal experience of all who have been liberated from the bondage of sin, but there are others in the world, who are still unsaved, and need this same change in their lives, so Jesus told this new convert, "*...Go home to thy friends, and tell them how great things the Lord hath done for thee, and hath had compassion on thee*" (St. Mark 5:19b). Jesus took care of this new convert at a distance, and He will do the same for us, when we are obedient to His commands.

The greatest proof of our love for God is our obedience. Jesus told His disciples, "*If ye love me, keep my commandments*" (St. John 14:15). What did He command His followers? Listen to Acts 1:8, "*And being assembled together with them, commanded them that they should not depart from Jerusalem, but wait for the promise of the Father, which saith He, ye have heard of me. For John truly baptized with water; but ye shall be baptized with the*

Holy Spirit not many days hence" (Acts 1:4-5). As a result of this experience they were to be witnesses "*unto the uttermost part of the earth*" (Acts 1:8).

We are prone to take for granted that most men know the basics of our Christian faith, but it is not so, even here in America. Years ago in one of my pastorates, I contacted a young boy on the street and invited him to our church. After talking awhile, he asked me, "What time does the show start?" But there are many adults groping in darkness, who are just as ignorant of the soul saving message we have to offer.

Again I say the greatest proof of our love for Jesus is to obey Him by heeding His command for us to be filled with the Holy Spirit, and then become a new "*threshing instrument*" (Isaiah 41:15) in His hands, and go forth to reach a lost and dying world for Christ.

Sing Unto The Lord
(Psalm 30:4a)

Take my life, and let it be consecrated, Lord, to Thee.
Take my hands, and let them move
At the impulse of Thy love,
At the impulse of Thy love.[1]

Verse to Memorize: *He that goeth forth and weepeth, bearing precious seed, shall doubtless come again with rejoicing, bringing his sheaves with him* (Psalm 126:6).

A Time to Rejoice

Background Scripture: St. Luke 2:8-11

And there were in the same country shepherds abiding in the field, keeping watch over their flock by night. And, lo, the angel of the Lord came upon them, and the glory of the Lord shone round about them: and they were sore afraid. And the angel said unto them, fear not: for, behold, I bring you good tidings of great joy, which shall be to all people. For unto you is born this day in the city of David a Saviour, which is Christ the Lord **(St. Luke 2:8-11).**

The message the angel delivered to the fearful shepherds was not a message of doom, but tidings of great joy to all people. The English word gospel is derived from the Anglo-Saxon gospel, which meant good tidings.

There was never, nor will there ever be such good news delivered to this lost, suffering planet than the fact that God, through Christ's sacrifice for our sins, has given the human race a second chance in order to recover our lost paradise. This world we know is a lost world. We say people will be lost, but outside of Christ, men are lost now.

The message of the entire Bible is one to "fear not" for all who have taken refuge in the true and living God. The Psalmist said, "*He shall not be afraid of evil tidings: his heart is fixed, trusting in the Lord*" (Psalm 112:7).

It was during the time of the lengthy illness and death of my beloved wife, that God gave me a verse that strengthened me while going through deep waters. It was Psalm 27:1, "*The Lord is my light and my salvation, whom shall I fear? the Lord is the strength of my life; of whom shall I be afraid*?" This promise, though given to me over twenty years ago, remains to give me strength as I continue in my pilgrimage to a better world.

When God's word admonishes us to fear God; it is in reference to our showing reverence to our Creator, but not a slavish carnal fear that brings torment. In contrast those who reject Christ and His offer of pardon, have every reason to fear. In Hebrews 10:31 we read, *"It is a fearful thing to fall into the hands of the living God."*

The good news is that provision has been made by Christ's sacrifice for our sins, that all may be delivered from carnal fear. If you have not experienced this deliverance, why not come now to Jesus Christ, who says…"*him that cometh to me I will in no wise cast out*" (St. John 6:37b).

Sing unto the Lord
(Psalm 30:4a)

Joy to the world! the Lord is come;
Let earth receive her King.
Let every heart prepare Him room.
And heaven and nature sing.[1]

Verse to Memorize: *I sought the Lord, and He heard me, and delivered me from all my fears* (Psalm 34:4).

UNLIMITED LOVE

Background Scripture: St. John 3:1-21

***For God so loved the world, that He gave His only begotten Son, that whosoever believeth in Him should not perish, but have everlasting life* (St. John 3:16).**

God does not attempt to elaborate concerning His love for a lost world in giving His only begotten Son as a sacrifice for our sin. He leaves the fact for men and angels to contemplate and revel in throughout all eternity, by merely using the little two lettered word "so" loved. According to God's word, the angels are not able to fathom such love and the depths for which God condescends in order to save us lost human beings. As St. Peter writes about the gospel being preached, he says, "*...which things the angels desire to look into*" (I Peter 1:12b).

Years ago, I read an account of a young officer who sacrificed his life in order to save his buddies. When the enemy cast a grenade into the trench, he immediately covered the deadly weapon with his own body. His body absorbed the full force of the explosion and he died, but his friends lived. Surely that was a display of love.

But, I know of a greater love. This young soldier died in order to save his friends, but I know One who sacrificed His life for men who "*despised and rejected*" (Isaiah 53:3) Him. "*For scarcely for a righteous man will one die: yet peradventure for a good man some would even dare to die. But God commendeth His love toward us, in that, while we were yet sinners, Christ died for us*" (Romans 5:7-8).

Let us not crucify Jesus Christ afresh (Hebrew 6:6) by neglecting such love, but accept God's Gift and be thankful.

Sing unto the Lord
(Psalm 30:4a)

That God should love a sinner such as I,
Should yearn to change my sorrow into bliss,
Nor rest till He had planned to bring me nigh,
How wonderful is love like this![1]

Verse to Memorize: *Behold, what manner of love the Father hath bestowed upon us, that we should be called the sons of God: therefore the world knoweth us not, because it knew Him not* (I John 3:1).

The Basic Need of the Church

Background Scripture: Acts 1-2

***But ye shall receive power, after that the Holy Ghost is come upon you: and ye shall be witnesses unto Me both in Jerusalem, and in Judea, and in Samaria, and unto the uttermost part of the earth* (Acts 1:8).**

This verse is the key to the book of Acts. All the miracles and mighty works that follow happened as a result of that which took place in the upper room, when the Holy Spirit cleansed and empowered the early church to evangelize the whole world.

Jesus told His disciples that it was "*expedient for you that I go away*" (John 16:7) in order that He might send the Comforter unto them, and as a result of His coming the disciples would be enabled to do even greater works than Christ did while on earth, because Jesus would ascend unto His Father.

We see these "greater works" reenacted whenever God's people tarry for their personal Pentecost. John Wesley's Journal reads much like the book of Acts. Why? It was because these early Methodists settled for nothing less than the baptism of the Holy Spirit and fire in their personal experience, and the same will happen in any age whenever we meet the conditions, for "*Jesus Christ is the same yesterday, and today, and for ever*" (Hebrews 13:8).

The great need of the Church today is to tarry for the baptism of the Holy Spirit, otherwise our words will fall on the ears of the lost as "*sounding brass, or a tinkling cymbal*" (I Corinthians 13:1b). John the Baptist preached, saying, *"I indeed baptize you with water unto repentance: but He that cometh after me is mightier than I, whose shoes I am not worthy to bear: He shall baptize you with the Holy Ghost, and with fire*" (Matthew 3:11).

When a church fails to make progress, it appears almost inevitable that God's people begin to look for better buildings, methods, and entertainment in order to fill the vacuum. Sometimes we need to change our methods, and build better and larger buildings in order that the church may grow; but the problem usually is the fact that the church has lost its first love, and no longer has the power that comes from the baptism of the Holy Spirit.

There is an illustration given of a train that came to a stop. The anxious passengers wondered what could be the trouble. There was no station, no water tank, but there they stood. Some went forward to the engine and made inquiry. "Haven't you got any water?" asked one. "Yes," replied the engineer, "but it's not boiling."[1]

This experience is not for a select few, but for all. "*For the promise is unto you, and to your children, and to all that are afar off, even as many as the Lord our God shall call*" (Acts 2:39). This experience brings soul health. Come, and you will not be disappointed.

Sing unto the Lord
(Psalm 30:4a)

Bring your empty earthen vessels, clean through Jesus precious blood.
Come, ye needy, one and all;
And in human consecration wait before the throne of God
Till the Holy Ghost shall fall.[2]

Verse to Memorize: *And, behold, I send the promise of my Father upon you: but tarry ye in the city of Jerusalem, until ye be endued with power from on high* (Luke 24:49).

"More Than Conquerors"

Background Scripture: Romans 8:31-39

***For I am persuaded that neither death, nor life, nor angels, nor principalities, nor powers, nor things present, nor things to come, Nor height, nor depth, nor any other creature, shall be able to separate us from the love of God, which is in Christ Jesus our Lord* (Romans 8:38-39).**

St. Paul is not writing as a novice, but as a veteran who had suffered much as God used him for the advancement of His kingdom on earth. In speaking of Paul, Jesus said, "*For I will shew him how great things he must suffer for my name's sake*" (Acts 9:16). Later in life the apostle enumerates a lengthy list of the hardships he endured as found in II Corinthians 11:23-28.

Through Jesus Christ, God has made ample provision for all Christian pilgrims, that we may overcome all obstacles placed in our way as we press forward to that celestial city. Satan's power is limited and always subject to God's authority. Before Satan could tempt Job, he had to get permission from God. (Job 1:12)

Satan tempts us in order to destroy us, but God permits temptation in order to strengthen us, and fit us for even greater service. It is not enough to endure temptation, but we must use it for the purpose, which God has in mind. Paul writes that God "*...comforteth us in all our tribulation, that we may be able to comfort them which are in any trouble, by the comfort wherewith we ourselves are comforted of God*" (II Corinthians 1:4b).

As we travel the highways, we sometimes notice before crossing a stream or river, a sign indicating the load limit of that particular bridge. Even so, God knows the load limit of each of His followers. Listen to I Corinthians 10:13. "*There hath no temptation taken you but such as is common to man: but God is faithful, who will not suffer you to be tempted above that ye are able; but will with the temptation also make a way to escape, that ye may be able to bear it.*"

It appears that God takes special notice of those faithful servants, whom He knows can be trusted to carry extraordinary burdens. It was so in the case of Job. We read in Job 1:8, "*And the Lord said unto Satan, Hast thou considered my servant Job, that there is none like him in the earth, a perfect and an upright man, one that feareth God, and escheweth evil?*"

There is an illustration given of Napoleon inspecting his troops before the great battle, which was impending. Turning from a mass of undisciplined, inexperienced men before him, he said to one of his generals, "These men I know nothing about." Then as his eye ran over a body of men who had been with him for a short time and knew something of march, bivouac, and battlefield, he said, "These men I think I can trust." Finally he turned to a division of troops who had been with him in all his campaigns. They were veterans of his army. They had been baptized in blood and fire in many a fierce and deadly struggle. As they stood before him with set lips and stern countenances, ready and waiting for the onset of the coming battle, the great commander turned from them with a heart pulsating with pride and confidence, and said quietly to his officers, "These men I know I can trust."[1]

Are we willing to become such soldiers in the army of the Lord?

Sing unto the Lord
(Psalm 30:4a)

Tho the angry surges roll on my tempest driven soul,
I am peaceful, for I know, Wildly though the winds may blow,
I've an anchor safe and sure, That can evermore endure.[2]

Verse to Memorize: *Many are the afflictions of the righteous: but the Lord delivereth him out of them all* (Psalm 34:19).

"A Vessel unto Honour"*

Background Scripture: I Corinthians 6:9-20

***What? know ye not that your body is the temple of the Holy Ghost which is in you, which ye have of God, and ye are not your own? For ye are bought with a price: therefore glorify God in your body, and in your spirit, which are God's* (I Corinthians 6:19-20).**

It was while being examined by a physician and we were trying to decide upon the best treatment for my illness, that the doctor said, "It is your body." Although I understand the reasoning of the physician, I have to disagree with the statement that I own my body. For the scripture says, "*ye are not your own*" (I Corinthians 6:19b).

It is true God has given us the freedom of choice as to whether we use our body in a destructive way or surrender ourselves so that the Holy Spirit takes His rightful place and our bodies become the "*temple of the Holy Ghost*" (v 19). We are free to choose, but not free when it comes to reaping the consequences of that choice. Listen to God's word, *"I call heaven and earth to record this day against you, that I have set before you life and death, blessing and cursing: therefore choose life, that both thou and thy seed may live"* (Deuteronomy 30:19).

Adam Clarke comments, "As truly as the living God dwelt in the Mosaic Tabernacle and in the Temple of Solomon, so truly does the Holy Ghost dwell in the souls of genuine Christians; and as the Temple and all its utensils were holy, separated from all common and profane uses and dedicated, alone to the service of God, so the bodies of genuine Christians are holy, and all their members should be employed in the service of God alone."[1]

This being true, then we should respond by taking care of the body in a manner that corresponds with the dignity God has endowed us with.

We need to discipline the body. Even St. Paul, as great a saint as he was, found it necessary to discipline the body, and said, "*But*

*A phrase found in II Timothy 2:21

I keep under my body, and bring it into subjection: lest that by any means, when I have preached to others, I myself should be a castaway" (I Corinthians 9:27).

It means we should clothe the body "*in modest apparel*" (I Timothy 2:9). Also, the body should be kept clean and well groomed. Although the heart may be clean and filled with the Holy Ghost, it is a poor testimony to the world, if our bodies and homes display filth. As God's people we should do all in our power to be healthy by practicing that which contributes to a healthy body. In so doing, we find it adds to our being better enabled to resist "*the wiles of the devil*" (Ephesians 6:11b).

Since we belong to God both by right of creation and by right of redemption, let us surrender all to Him, and in so doing we find that "*the peace of God, which passeth all understanding, shall keep your hearts and minds through Christ Jesus*" (Philippians 4:7b).

Sing unto the Lord
(Psalm 30:4a)

Let my hands perform His bidding;
Let my feet run in His ways;
Let my eyes see Jesus only;
Let my lips speak forth His praise.[2]

Verse to Memorize: *For ye are bought with a price: therefore glorify God in your body, and in your spirit, which are God's* (I Corinthians 6:20).

A Clean Heart

Having therefore these promises, dearly beloved, let us cleanse ourselves from all filthiness of the flesh and spirit, perfecting holiness in the fear of God **(II Corinthians 7:1).**

One of the great leaders of our denomination was once asked the question as to which is greater sin, that of the flesh or the sin of the spirit. Without hesitation, he answered that sin of the spirit is worse.

Sin is deadly, however it manifests itself. Of course, all sins come from a corrupt carnal heart. The heart must first be changed in order for one to produce the fruit of the Spirit.

But why is the sin of the spirit, such as envy, hate and pride, etc. even more to be on guard against than sins of the flesh? It is because the sins of the spirit are not always easily detected.

It is with sorrow that I remember how my wife was sick, and after a physical examination, the physician pronounced her healthy. Soon after she was diagnosed as having a malignant ovarian tumor. Why was the physician unable to find the cause of her malady? It was simply because an ovarian tumor is a soft tumor and not easily detected and diagnosed.

So it is with the sins of the spirit. For a while an individual may be festering inwardly with all kinds of corruption, yet appear as a holy person. Jesus rebuked the scribes and Pharisees for this very thing, saying they were "*...like unto whited sepulchres, which indeed appear beautiful outward, but are within full of dead men's bones, and of all uncleanness*" (Matthew 23:27b).

The text says we should "*cleanse ourselves.*" We realize it is impossible for us to save ourselves, but the command means we should do our part by surrendering to the cure our Great Physician has in store for us. Then we are spiritually healthy.

God wants to restore His image in each of us until people who observe us will be forced to say as they did of Peter and John: "*they took knowledge of them, that they had been with Jesus*" (Acts 4:13b).

Sing unto the Lord
(Psalm 30:4a)

Lord Jesus, I long to be perfectly whole;
I want Thee forever, to live in my soul.
Break down every idol, cast out every foe.
Now wash me and I shall be whiter than snow.[1]

Verse to Memorize: *But if we walk in the light, as He is in the light, we have fellowship one with another, and the blood of Jesus Christ His Son cleanseth us from all sin* (I John 1:7).

Saved by Grace Alone

Knowing that a man is not justified by the works of the law, but by the faith of Jesus Christ, even we have believed in Jesus Christ, that we might be justified by the faith of Christ, and not by the works of the law: for by the works of the law shall no flesh be justified **(Galatians 2:16).**

After heeding the call of the Holy Spirit to seek Christ, the first step in repenting is to realize there is nothing whatsoever one can do to atone for his sin, even as Jesus told of the two debtors, "*And when they had nothing to pay, he frankly forgave them both*" (Luke 7:42a). Our reasonings and struggles, good works, etc., will never atone for our sin, but rather hinder in our approach to God. It is by grace and grace alone that we are saved. The hymn writer, Toplady, expresses it clearly in saying, "Could my tears forever flow, Could my zeal no languor know, These for sin, could not atone; Thou must save, and Thou alone."[1]

I believe it was Gypsy Smith who relates how a son tried to save his drowning mother. His mother would not relax and cease from trying to struggle and save herself, consequently her son was unable to rescue her, and she died. After her death, the son lamented how he would have saved the life of his mother, if she had only allowed him to.

Likewise, men have many ways of trying to gain entrance to that City. I know a kind lady who took stray dogs and cats to her home. She told my son she did it so she would go to heaven. The Christian must and will do good deeds, for God's Word says, "*...I will that thou affirm constantly, that they which have believed in God might be careful to maintain good works*" (Titus 3:8 part). In that sense James writes about Abraham saying, "*Ye see then how that by works a man is justified, and not by faith only*" (James 2:24).

But good works will not atone for sin. Jesus says, "*I am the door: by Me if any man enter in, he shall be saved, and shall go in and out, and find pasture*" (St. John 10:9).

The Galatians had received the Spirit by faith in the finished work of Jesus Christ on the cross. When Jesus cried from the cross, "*It is finished*" there was nothing to be added or nothing to be taken away. But these people were trying to add to the finished work of our Saviour by adding the law. Paul writes, "*Are ye so foolish? having begun in the Spirit, are ye now made perfect by the flesh?*" (Galatians 3:3). This doesn't mean the Christian is without law; for Jesus came not to destroy, but to fulfill the law, consequently there is no other sacrifice for sin.

When one seeks to be saved, Satan will resist with all the weapons he has at his disposal. Just the moment when the seeker's faith has reached out to touch the hem of Christ's garment, the devil will suggest something more one must do, and listening to this suggestion will cause the seeker to relapse, and fall back into darkness. These suggestions of Satan must be resisted, and with Job say "*though He slay me, yet will I trust Him*" (Job 13:15a). Then the victory comes, and the witness comes, if not at that moment, the witness of the Holy Spirit is sure to come to the trusting soul. The witness may come as you go about your daily routine. "*...the Lord, whom ye seek, shall suddenly come to His temple, ...*" (Malachi 3:1 part).

Sing unto the Lord
(Psalm 30:4a)

Oh, to grace how great a debtor
Daily I'm constrained to be!
Let that grace, now like a fetter,
Bind my yielded heart to Thee.
Let me know Thee in thy fullness;
Guide me by Thy mighty hand
Till, transformed, in Thine own image
In Thy presence I shall stand.[2]

Verse to Memorize: *For what the law could not do, in that it was weak through the flesh, God sending His own Son in the likeness of sinful flesh, and for sin, condemned sin in the flesh: That the righteousness of the law might be fulfilled in us, who walk not after the flesh, but after the Spirit* (Romans 8:3-4).

EQUIPPED FOR SPIRITUAL WARFARE

Background Scripture: Ephesians 6:10-20

***Put on the whole armour of God, that ye may be able to stand against the wiles of the devil. For we wrestle not against flesh and blood, but against principalities, against powers, against the rulers of the darkness of this world, against spiritual wickedness in high places* (Ephesians 6:11-12).**

We as Christians are engaged in a spiritual warfare, though invisible, on the outcome of which our eternal destiny rests. According to the scripture, we are surrounded not only by good angels sent from God, who guard and fight on our behalf, but also by the fallen angels under the leadership of Satan, which are warring against us. Adam Clarke comments, "The apostle considers every Christian as having a warfare to maintain against numerous, powerful, and subtle foes; and that therefore they would need much strength, much courage, complete armor, and skill to use it."[1] If we become lax in our devotional life and fail to keep the whole armor of God on, then we become easy prey for the enemy. We are no match for the superhuman powers of the evil forces arrayed against us under Satan, but when we rely on God, "*we are more than conquerors through Him that loved us*" (Romans 8:37b).

The best defense for the Christian soldier is to be on the offensive. God's word says, "*Be not overcome of evil, but overcome evil with good*" (Romans 12:21). Our real enemy is not "*flesh and blood,*" signifying human beings like ourselves, "*but principalities, powers, rulers of darkness of this world, and spiritual wickedness in high places*" (Eph. 6:12). So Jesus admonishes us to be on the offensive when He says, "*But I say unto you, Love your enemies, bless them that curse you, do good to them that hate you, and pray for them which despitefully use you, and persecute you*" (Matthew 5:44).

God tells us to resist Satan. Listen to James 4:7. "*Submit yourselves therefore to God. Resist the devil, and he will flee from you.*" I remember hearing our late District Superintendent, Dr. Harvey S. Galloway, saying that the Christian doesn't have to be kicked about like a football by Satan. An evangelist and I were making a call in a certain home, and when leaving, a dog came running and chasing after us. I decided to get on the offensive and turning about, I ran straight toward my would-be enemy, and it was really comical to see that dog run away from us. We cannot combat the evil one in our own strength, but in the name of our Great Captain, who overcame Satan by His death and resurrection, we can conquer all the forces that assail us.

St. Paul writes, "*I can do all things through Christ which strengtheneth me*" (Philippians 4:13). This strength is available to all who have placed their trust in Christ.

Sing unto the Lord
(Psalm 30:4a) *Soldiers of Immanuel go forward in His name,*
Holy warfare waging, powers of sin engaging.
Lift His royal standard and His truth divine proclaim,
Till the world shall own Him King.[2]

Verse to Memorize: *Thou therefore endure hardness, as a good soldier of Jesus Christ* (II Timothy 2:3).

Death as an Asset

Background Scripture: Philippians 1:21-26

For to me to live is Christ, and to die is gain **(Philippians 1:21).**

In writing to the Corinthian church, St. Paul enumerates the things God's people can lay hold on as their possession. Among the various things listed, we find that death is mentioned as one of the things that a Christian should prize. It is true God's word speaks of death as our "*last enemy*" (I Corinthians 15:26), but we also read, "*Precious in the sight of the Lord is the death of His saints*" (Psalm 116:15).

With the Apostle death was not the matter of importance, but Paul's one overwhelming goal and ambition was that "*...Christ shall be magnified in my body, whether it be by life, or by death*" (Philippians 1:20b). This should also be our desire.

The Apostle, if left for him to decide, was perplexed as to suffering on in this world or to depart and be with Christ. He writes, "*For I am in a strait betwixt two, having a desire to depart, and to be with Christ; which is far better: Nevertheless to abide in the flesh is more needful for you*" (Philippians 1:23-24). Adam Clarke makes the following comment, "It appears to be a metaphor taken from the commander of a vessel, in a foreign port, who feels a strong desire 'to set sail,' and to get to his own country and family, but this desire is counter balanced by a conviction that the general interests of the voyage may be best answered by his longer stay in the port where his vessel now rides."[1]

Perhaps the reason many do not share St. Paul's desire to depart and to be with Christ, is that life on earth has become too attractive, having not experienced even in a small degree the sufferings of St. Paul as we read of in II Corinthians 11:23.

In our affluent culture we sing, "A tent or a cottage, why should I care? They're building a palace for me over there!"[2] But many professed followers of Christ can sing the words with no anticipation of the blessing to come, for they have already built their palaces here on earth. Suffering gave birth to many Negro spirituals for these people suffered much. No wonder when beaten, overworked and separated from their families, they would sing "Swing low, sweet chariot, coming for to carry me home."

Nevertheless, we all, to some extent, suffer in one-way or another in this present fallen world. We read, "*For we know that the whole creation groaneth and travaileth in pain together until now. And not only they, but ourselves also, which have the first fruits of the Spirit, even ourselves groan within ourselves waiting for the adoption, to wit, the redemption of our body.*" (Romans 8:22-23)

But there is a better world for those who in Christ have made the necessary preparation. Years ago, I heard an older preacher say that he had loved ones here and loved ones on the other side, and he didn't know where he wanted to be. Really, Christ makes it heaven, whether here on earth or in our final abode. Let us nestle up closer to the breast of Jesus like John (St. John 13:25) and all will be well whether we live or die.

Sing unto the Lord
(Psalm 30:4a)

Living for Jesus thru earth's little while,
My dearest treasure, the light of His smile
Seeking the lost ones. He died to redeem,
Bringing the weary to find rest in Him![3]

Verse to Memorize: *But as it is written, Eye hath not seen, nor ear heard, neither have entered into the heart of man, the things which God hath prepared for them that love Him* (I Corinthians 2:9).

Heavenly Minded

Background Scripture: Colossians 3:1-11

If ye then be risen with Christ, seek those things which are above, where Christ sitteth on the right hand of God. Set your affection on things above, not on things on the earth **(Colossians 3:1-2).**

Paul was in prison when he wrote this letter to the Colossians. Binding him in prison could not separate or take from him his true source of joy and happiness, for Paul's entire life was so surrendered to God, that God's plan being fulfilled caused him to be content wherever he was placed.

We as God's children should follow the example of the Apostle in setting our affections on things above and "*...earnestly contend for the faith...*" (Jude 3). We who know Christ as our Lord and Saviour, have experienced the reality of the life that we now possess in Christ, as well as that which is to come in a better world. Therefore we are willing and want Jesus Christ to be our only source of happiness. We have sold all we have in order to secure the "*one pearl of great price*" (Matthew 13:46).

When Jesus Christ is made the very center of our life, we will not look back or long for the old life, remembering the words of Jesus, "*...No man, having put his hand to the plough, and looking back, is fit for the kingdom of God*" (Luke 9:62b).

Occasionally, one hears professed Christians testify as to what sacrifice and what cost it was to them in order to become followers of Christ. God's word pictures His people, the church, as the bride and our Saviour as the bridegroom. In Revelations 21:9 we see this: "*...Come, I will show you the bride, the Lamb's wife.*"

What would an onlooker think if after a beautiful wedding, the bride would go about telling all her acquaintances of what it cost her to marry her husband? She might say something like this, "I had to give up Henry, Joe and Jack and all of my old boyfriends, but oh! How I love my husband."

This may sound ridiculous, but it makes sense when we think of some of the testimonies we hear. If we really love our God, it will be an all-consuming love that literally blots out all our old affections for the genuine affection we have for Christ our Bridegroom.

Sing unto the Lord (Psalm 30:4a)

My Jesus I love Thee; I know Thou art mine.
For Thee all the follies of sin I resign.
My gracious Redeemer, my Saviour art Thou.
If ever I loved Thee, my Jesus 'tis now.[1]

Verses to Memorize: *Again the kingdom of heaven is like unto a merchant man, seeking goodly pearls: Who, when he had found one pearl of great price, went and sold all that he had, and bought it* (Matthew 13:45-46).

The Central Message of the Bible

Background Scripture: I Thessalonians 5:14-28

***And the very God of peace sanctify you wholly; and I pray God your whole spirit and soul and body be preserved blameless unto the coming of our Lord Jesus Christ* (I Thessalonians 5:23).**

God's word makes it clear that it is God's will that we should be sanctified wholly. In I Thessalonians 4:3a we read, "*For this is the will of God, even your sanctification…*" If then it is God's will, He will perform that which He wills, if we respond to His call to holiness and surrender unconditionally. In the context we read, "*Faithful is He that calleth you* [to holiness], *who also will do it"* (I Thessalonians 5:24).

Some have attempted to build an entire doctrine around some isolated portion of Scripture, failing to read all God has to say on the subject. But we find the entire message of the Bible has one goal in view, and that is to restore fallen man to the image of God in which he was originally created (Genesis 1:2a). Jesus in the Sermon on the mountain commands, "*Be ye therefore perfect, even as your Father which is in heaven is perfect*" (Matthew 5:48). We still have our faults, but the heart made perfect through the atoning blood of Jesus Christ will be so perfected in love that we will love God with all our heart, and love our neighbor as our self. Also, being motivated by love, we will not willfully sin against our God, or our neighbor. This is holiness.

In verse 23a we read, "*And the very God of peace…*" which signifies that God desires that we enjoy the serenity and peace that God Himself experiences. Listen to the prophecy of Isaiah, "*And the work of righteousness shall be peace; and the effect of righteousness quietness and assurance forever*" (Isaiah 32:17).

The reason mankind is so troubled and restless is that fallen man is under Satan's control until he is liberated, and unshackled, thus being set free by the blood of Jesus Christ. The Scriptures portrays a black picture of fallen depraved man in Isaiah 57:20-21. "*But the wicked are like the troubled sea, when it cannot rest, whose waters cast up mire and dirt. There is no peace, saith my God, to the wicked.*"

In contrast to those outside of Christ, we find the peace Jesus Christ offered to all in St. John 14:27. "*Peace I leave with you, My peace I give unto you: not as the world giveth, give I unto you. Let not your heart be troubled, neither let it be afraid.*"

But the Holy Spirit cannot enter a filthy heart. We must first come to Christ confessing our sins, believing He died and arose for our justification. In Romans 10:9, God's word says, "*That if thou shalt confess with thy mouth the Lord Jesus, and shalt believe in thine heart that God hath raised Him from the dead, thou shalt be saved.*"

After this we are candidates for the further work of being filled with the Holy Spirit. After this takes place, our human part is to consecrate our all to God, and God's work is to sanctify us wholly.

Sing unto the Lord
(Psalm 30:4a)

It is for us all today
If we trust and truly pray.
Consecrate to Christ your all,
And upon the Saviour call.
Bless God, it is for us all today.[1]

Verse to Memorize: *I indeed baptize you with water unto repentance: but He that cometh after me is mightier than I, whose shoes I am not worthy to bear: He shall baptize you with the Holy Ghost, and with fire* (Matthew 3:11).

Further Holiness Teaching

***But we are bound to give thanks always to God for you brethren beloved of the Lord, because God hath from the beginning chosen you to salvation through sanctification of the Spirit and belief of the truth: Whereunto He called you by our gospel, to the obtaining of the glory of our Lord Jesus Christ* (II Thessalonians 2:13-14).**

The church at Thessalonica was an exemplary church. We do not read of such problems as existed at Corinth. St. Paul speaks of their "*work of faith, and labor of love, and patience of hope in our Lord Jesus Christ, in the sight of God and our Father*" (I Thessalonians 1:3b). He speaks of them as "*ensamples to all that believe in Macedonia and Achaia*" (I Thessalonians 1:7b). Furthermore the Apostle writes of their faith and missionary effort.

Yet, Paul continues to emphasize the need of a further work of grace, declaring this to be the purpose of God in the call. God's purpose from the beginning was to provide salvation for both Jew and Gentile that would restore fallen man to the image of God. Even after one has been baptized with the Holy Spirit, he needs to hear the message of holiness proclaimed as in this account.

In his first letter Paul assured this church he was praying for their sanctification (I Thessalonians 5:23). Then after a lapse of time, the Apostle writes this second letter. It would be interesting to know what the church wrote when they answered his first letter, before Paul wrote his second epistle. However, we can conjecture somewhat of that which they wrote in the same manner as we listen to one side of a telephone conversation; and can know what the other party is saying.

In answering their letter, Paul writes, "*We are bound to thank God always for you, brethren, as it is meet, because that your faith groweth exceedingly, and the charity of everyone of you all toward each other aboundeth*" (II Thessalonians 1:3).

So it appears that Paul's prayer had been answered that they might be sanctified wholly, but how do we know? We know their faith was growing exceedingly and their love for one another abounded. The fruit of their lives was evident that they had walked in the light and had pressed on to holiness.

As pastors we know it is one thing to seek and find God in His fullness, but we also realize this experience must be maintained by feeding on the Word of God, prayer, faithfully attending church and by doing good to the souls and bodies of men, etc.

Paul writes, "*But the Lord is faithful, who shall stablish you, and keep you from evil*" (II Thessalonians 3:3). Yet, Paul heard of some (chapter 3:1) who were not working but were busybodies. Perhaps they, like some in our day, were expecting the soon return of Christ, and thought it was no longer necessary to work. It has been said, "an idle mind is the devil's workshop." Holiness and laziness are incompatible. Then this lifestyle led to a disorderly conduct (II Thessalonians 3:11) and they became busybodies. Paul didn't recommend casting them out of the church, but he wrote, "*Now them that are such we command and exhort by our Lord Jesus Christ, that with quietness they work, and eat their own bread*" (II Thessalonians 3:12). But if such people would not heed this command, a further step was to be taken as found in verses 14 and 15 that might restore them to the fold as a faithful follower of Christ.

So we see it is important to lead our people into the fullness of the blessing and then help them to grow in the knowledge of our Lord and Saviour, Jesus Christ.

Sing unto the Lord
(Psalm 30:4a)

I'm pressing on the upward way.
New heights I'm gaining every day,
Still praying as I onward bound,
"Lord plant my feet on higher ground."[1]

Verse to Memorize: *I press toward the mark for the prize of the high calling of God in Christ Jesus* (Philippians 3:14).

CONTENTMENT

Background Scripture: I Timothy 6:6-21

But godliness with contentment is great gain. For we brought nothing into this world, and it is certain we can carry nothing out.And having food and raiment let us be therewith content **(I Timothy 6:6-8).**

Our Lord and Saviour Jesus Christ strikes at the heart of the matter of contentment when He says, "*...Take heed and beware of covetousness: for a man's life consisteth not in the abundance of things which he possesseth*" (Luke 12:15b). All things are temporal and will soon pass away, even as the earth upon which we dwell.

The rich man made the same mistake that the majority of people make today when he thought he could feed his never dying soul on the crumbs of this material world. He said, "*And I will say to my soul, 'Soul, thou hast much goods laid up for many years; take thine ease, eat, drink, and be merry*'" (Luke 12:19). In His temptation Jesus resisted Satan by the word of God, saying, "*...It is written, Man shall not live by bread alone, but by every word that proceedeth out of the mouth of God*" (Matthew 4:4b).

Adam Clarke writes, "The word we translate raiment signifies 'covering' in general and here means house or lodging as well as clothing."[1] Today we live in a more complex society and have other necessities, but the principle remains that we should be content, with having the necessary things of life, and not be seeking for the luxuries that will never satisfy. When we have the life of Christ in the soul, we are satisfied, but without this life, we will never be happy regardless of how many "toys" we own.

A rich man confided in me, saying how difficult it was for him to manage his possessions. He served God and gave much in the building of God's kingdom; yet, he found a problem in handling his possessions. This reminds me of the words of Jesus when He said to His disciples, "*Verily I say unto you, that a rich man shall hardly enter into the kingdom of heaven*" (Matthew 19:23b). Jesus went on to explain in Matthew 19:26 that it is possible, but in verse 24 explains that it is with difficulty. The antidote is found in I Timothy 6:17-19 where we read, "*Charge them that are rich in this world, that they be not high-minded, nor trust in uncertain riches, but in the living God, who giveth us richly all things to enjoy; That they do good, that they be rich in good works, ready to distribute, willing to communicate; Laying up in store for themselves a good foundation against the time to come, that they may lay hold on eternal life.*"

St. Paul suffered much as recorded in II Corinthians 11:23-29, yet, he writes, "*...for I have learned, in whatsoever state I am, therewith to be content*" (Philippians 4:11b). I also learned this lesson of contentment as a young man when my health failed, and I found myself seriously ill for a long period of time, dependent on the mercies of others. But God taught me lessons that have been a blessing to me during a long life. I learned to appreciate those things we take for granted. I enjoy fresh air and sunshine. I can say, "little is much when God is in it." Along with David, I can testify, "*I have been young, and now am old; yet have I not seen the righteous forsaken, nor his seed begging bread*" (Psalm 37:25).

Sing unto the Lord (Psalm 30:4a)

A tent or a cottage, why should I care?
They're building a palace for me over there!
Tho exiled from home, yet still I may sing:
"All glory to God, I'm a child of the King!"[2]

Verse to Memorize: *Remove far from me vanity and lies: give me neither poverty nor riches; feed me with food convenient for me* (Proverbs 30:8).

Overcoming Our Weaknesses

Background Scripture: II Timothy 1:1-14

***For God had not given us the spirit of fear; but of power, and of love, and of a sound mind* (II Timothy 1:7).**

God's word portrays both the virtues and the sins of the men and women found within the pages of the sixty-six books of the Bible. In writing biography, modern men may exalt the virtues of an individual while remaining silent about his failures and sins. But God gives us a complete picture of a man, not covering up for any, that we may follow the example set forth by the good, and be warned of the pitfalls of following the life-style of the wicked.

As we read the Bible, it is refreshing to find some men like Joseph, Samuel, Daniel, and others who served God with no marks against them. Also, the character of Timothy was above reproach. This young man was genuine and his Christian walk with God gave full proof of his conversion and of having been filled with the Holy Spirit. In writing to the Philippians, Paul mentions Timothy, saying, *"For I have no man like-minded, who will naturally care for your state. For all seek their own, not the things which are Jesus Christ's. But ye know the proof of him, that, as a son with the father, hath served with me in the gospel." (*Philippians 2:20-22)

Yet, in verse 6, Paul admonishes Timothy to *"stir up the gift of God, which is in thee by the putting on of my hands"* (II Timothy 1:6b). Adam Clarke comments, "The gift which Timothy had received was the Holy Spirit; and through Him a particular power to preach and defend the thruth."[1]

Notwithstanding all the virtues and the godly life of this fine young man, he had a lack in the form of a weakness that must be overcome if he were to make full proof of his ministry. This weakness consisted of fear, which appears to be a natural timidity and retiring nature. This was not carnal fear, for *"perfect love casteth out fear"* (I John 4:18). Timothy had already experienced this "perfect love" when baptized with the Holy Spirit and fire.

But, we need to continue to grow in the grace and knowledge of our Lord and Saviour Jesus Christ after our hearts are cleansed from sin.

Perhaps we all have weaknesses in one form or another, but God enables the one whose heart is pure, washed in the blood of Christ, to become strong in the very area where he feels his weakness. Oh! how patient God is as He continues to help us to become more like Jesus.

Sing Unto the Lord
(Psalm 30:4a)

More about Jesus would I know,
More of His holy will discern;
Spirit of God, my Teacher be,
Showing the things of Christ to me.[2]

A Look at Ourselves in Retrospect

Background Scripture: Titus 3:1-7

For we ourselves also were sometimes foolish, disobedient, deceived, serving divers lusts and pleasures, living in malice and envy, hateful, and hating one another **(Titus 3:3).**

Our Lord and Saviour Jesus Christ, and the Apostle Paul both warn us concerning the dangers of looking back to the life from which we have been delivered. Lot's wife is a classical example of this peril, for she had been warned not to look back after she was delivered from Sodom. Then we read, "*But his wife looked back from behind him, and she became a pillar of salt*" (Genesis 19:2b).

In looking back, there is the danger of temptation to return to the former life on one hand, or on the other hand to become weakened in our pursuit after holiness and the prize set before us as we dwell upon the sins and failures of the past which are covered by the blood of our precious Lord and Saviour Jesus Christ.

While not gazing too long at the past, the Word of God teaches us that we should never forget the great deliverance God wrought for us in Jesus Christ, when He lifted us out of the pit of sin and cleansed our carnal hearts. As David reflected on his deliverance, he writes, "*He brought me up also out of an horrible pit, out of the miry clay, and set my feet upon a rock, and established my goings*" (Psalm 40:2). St. Paul says, "*For I am the least of the apostles, that am not meet to be called an apostle, because I persecuted the church of God*" I Corinthians 15:9). Both David and Paul only looked on the past long enough to remember their deliverance, and it led them to an even greater appreciation of God's love in giving His only begotten Son for their redemption. Then they broke out in praise to God.

Likewise, Paul reminds Titus "*that we ourselves also were sometimes foolish, disobedient, deceived, serving divers lusts and pleasures, living in malice and envy, hateful, and hating one another*" (Titus 3:3).

So when we see people blinded and following the dead-end road of sin, we should remember, there we would be if it were not for the mercy and grace of God.

Years ago, I heard a great leader of our denomination say, "Every time I pray and begin telling God how great a sinner a man is, God points out my need." I think I get the message, for Jesus says, "*So likewise ye, when ye shall have done all those things which are commanded you, say, We are unprofitable servants: we have done that which was our duty to do" (Luke 17:10).*

Sing unto the Lord
(Psalm 30:4a)

I saw a Blood washed pilgrim, A sinner saved by grace,
Upon the King's great highway With peaceful shining face.
Temptations sore beset him, But nothing could affright.
He said: "The yoke is easy; The burden it is light."[1]

Verses to Memorize: *It is of the Lord's mercies that we are not consumed, because His compassions fail not. They are new every morning: great is Thy faithfulness* (Lamentations 3:22-23).

LOVE PREVAILING

Background Scripture: Philemon

Wherefore, though I might be much bold in Christ to enjoin thee that which is convenient, Yet for love's sake I rather beseech thee, being such an one as Paul the aged, and now also a prisoner of Jesus Christ. I beseech thee for my son Onesimus, whom I have begotten in my bonds **(Philemon 8-10).**

The entire book of Philemon consists of only twenty-five verses, which is a personal letter of St. Paul to his Christian brother Philemon, concerning Onesimus, a runaway slave of Philemon, who had escaped but was converted as Paul ministered to him, even though the Apostle was at this time in bonds (Verse 10).

Although a personal letter, the authenticity and the place of the book of Philemon in the sacred canon has never been doubted or disputed from Christian antiquity.

On what basis can a personal letter concerning slavery be of help to Christians where this evil institution has been abolished for many years? I feel sure that God in His wisdom designed this book to be included in the Holy Scriptures for the simple reason that there are principles here, which will never be outdated.

Paul had the authority to command Philemon to receive his now converted slave "*not now as a servant, but above a servant, a brother beloved*" (Verse 16a). But in verse 9, Paul writes, "*Yet for love's sake I rather beseech thee.*"

Any consideration shown to Onesimus by his master, which was forced and did not stem from love, would have been detrimental to Philemon's development in the Christian faith. Paul wanted this forgiveness to come from the heart out of love and not by command. God made man in His own image, and for that reason, we do not want forced love even as God gave us the freedom to love Him on a voluntary basis.

There is strength or force in love, which can and will break the hardest heart. It is not a short cut to a realized goal, but it is God's way, and God's ways always works. I can testify in my personal relations that love and patience can prevail against the seemingly unmovable situations we face in life.

We do not have any answer from Philemon to Paul, but we have every reason to assume that love prevailed and Paul's request to Philemon for Onesimus was granted.

Sing unto the Lord
(Psalm 30:4a)

It's just like Jesus to roll the clouds away.
It's just like Jesus to keep me day by day.
It's just like Jesus all along the way.
It's just like His great love.[1]

Verse to Memorize: *And above all things have fervent charity (love) among yourselves: for charity shall cover the multitude of sins* (I Peter 4:8).

The Necessity of Holiness

Background Scripture: Hebrews 12:14-24

Follow peace with all men, and holiness, without which no man shall see the Lord **(Hebrews 12:14).**

In his book, *Holiness Triumphant*, Dr. J. B. Chapman relates an incident that took place in the history of France when the young prince approached a village where he was met by a committee of the principle citizens. They told him it had been their great desire and full purpose to greet his coming with the sound of numerous artillery. "But", they said, "we have thirteen reasons for not doing this. The first reason is that we do not have any artillery." The prince was a practical man, so he stopped the recital, and said, "My dear friends, this first reason is quite sufficient, so you need not mention the other twelve."[1]

In like manner, the Bible mentions many reasons why we should be sanctified wholly, but this text is enough proof, for without holiness no man shall see the Lord. In this sense, to see the Lord means to enjoy His fellowship, and be fitted to commune with Him both in this life and in that world yet to come.

Everyone will see the Lord, but not all alike. In Revelations 1:7a, we read, "*Behold, He cometh with clouds; and every eye shall see Him, and they also which pierced Him: and all kindreds of the earth shall wail because of Him…*" Those whose hearts are not made pure by the shed blood of Christ, will know the fear of viewing Christ as we read, "*And the kings of the earth, and the great men, and the rich men, and the chief captains, and the mighty men, and every bondman, and every free man, hid themselves in the dens and in the mountains: And said to the mountains and rocks, Fall on us, and hide us from the face of Him that sitteth on the throne, and from the wrath of the Lamb: For the great day of His wrath is come; and who shall be able to stand?*" (Revelation 6:15-17)

Whether this judgment applied to the final judgment of Jerusalem, or to the day of judgment "*when God shall judge the secrets of men by*

Jesus Christ…" (part of Romans 1:16), the truth remains the same. We must have on the wedding garment of holiness as the necessary preparation to stand in God's holy presence and be admitted to heaven.

Sing unto the Lord (Psalm 30:4a)

"Called unto holiness," Children of light,
Walking with Jesus in garments of white;
Raiment unsullied, nor tarnished with sin;
God's Holy Spirit abiding within.[2]

Verse to Memorize: *Herein is our love made perfect, that we may have boldness in the day of judgment: because as He is, so are we in this world* (I John 4:17).

A Definition of Pure Religion

Background Scripture: James 1:26-27.

***Pure religion and undefiled before God and the Father is this, to visit the fatherless and widows in their affliction, and to keep himself unspotted from the world* (James 1:27).**

God is holy and the very essence of purity. Not only has provision been made through the atonement of Christ's shed blood that all "would be" followers of God must be holy and pure, but also God has called us to holiness, and demands that we conform to His image if we are to be His children. In I Peter 1:15-16, we read, "*But as He which hath called you is holy, so be ye holy in all manner of conversation; because it is written, 'Be ye holy; for I am holy.'*"

An earthly father is delighted when he is told that his son is the "spitting image of his father." Likewise, in the moral realm, God takes pleasure in those whose hearts are washed in the blood of Christ, and the image of God thus restored in their lives.

This perfection is not angelic perfection or even Adamic perfection, but it merely consists of loving "*...the Lord thy God with all thy heart, and with all thy soul, and with all thy mind*" (Matthew 22:37b) and to "love thy neighbor as thyself" (Matthew 22:39b). The quantity of our love will not equal that of God, but the quality will be the same. Recently I received a gift of a Skyscan Atomic Clock with outdoor wireless temperature. This clock receives the exact time signal from radio station WWVB in Fort Collins, CO which derives its signal from NIST Atomic Clock in Boulder, CO. Our clock always displays the correct time, because it continually receives the signal from the atomic clock in Boulder, CO. Even so, the one filled with the Holy Spirit will naturally display the life of Christ even as Peter and John when the people looking on, "*...took knowledge of them, that they had been with Jesus*" (Acts 4"13b).

We as human beings still have weaknesses and faults, but our love for God and our fellow men will so resemble the love of God, that we would rather die than to willfully sin against God. We will feel like

Joseph, when solicited by Potiphar's wife, he said, "...*how then can I do this great wickedness, and sin against God?*" (Genesis 39:9b)

This definition of pure religion refers to the results of a cleansed heart, manifesting itself in practical everyday Christian living. Visiting the fatherless and widows, and attempting in one's own strength to keep unspotted from the world will never redeem us, "...*for by the works of the law shall no flesh be justified*" (Galatians 2:16b).

But good works and living clean in a sinful world will be the natural result and overflow of a clean heart "*filled with all the fullness of God*" (Ephesians 3:19b).

There is a sobering thought we must remember and that is on the great judgment day the only sins Jesus will mention are the sins of omission (see Matthew 25:35-46). Sins of commission and omission are the same, in that they stem from a defiled heart, but a great danger of the Holiness Movement is in failing to realize that sins of omission are just as devastating and damming as sins of commission (see Matthew 25:45-46). "*Therefore to him that knoweth to do good, and doeth it not, to him it is sin*" (James 4:17).

Sing unto the Lord (Psalm 30:4a)

I would be true, for there are those who trust me.
I would be pure, for there are those who care.
I would be strong, for there is much to suffer.
I would be brave, for there is much to dare.[1]

Verse to Memorize: *He hath shewed thee, O man, what is good; and what doth the Lord require of thee, but to do justly, and to love mercy, and to walk humbly with thy God?* (Micah 6:8)

A Sure Cure for Worry

Likewise, ye younger, submit yourselves unto the elder. Yea, all of you be subject one to another and be clothed with humility: for God resisteth the proud, and giveth grace to the humble. Humble yourselves therefore under the mighty hand of God, that He may exalt you in due time: Casting all your care upon Him for He careth for you **(I Peter 5:5-7).**

Various translations have rendered the word translated cares in the King James Version as anxieties. Either translation points us to the fact that God cares for us and invites us to cast all our concerns on Him.

The Holy Spirit must have directed St. Peter back to Psalm 55:2 as he wrote this Epistle, for there we read similar words, "*Cast thy burden upon the Lord, and He shall sustain thee*." God inspired St. Paul to write the same message in Philippians 4:6 where we read, "*Be careful for nothing: but in everything by prayer and supplication with thanksgiving let your requests be made known unto God*." Adam Clarke comments on this verse; "Be not anxiously solicitous. Do not give place to carking care, let what will occur; for anxiety cannot change the state or condition of anything from bad to good, but will infallibly injure your own souls."[1] Our Saviour says, "*Which of you by taking thought can add one cubit unto his stature*?" (Matthew 6:27)

The message on the bulletin board in front of a church must have been placed there by mistake. Instead of reading "Why worry when you can pray?" it said, "Why pray when you can worry?" The lady who read the message called the minister, so a correction could be made. In practical everyday living, many of us have the message in reverse.

But we do have recourse to prayer, and we should rely on God more than we often do.

Some of us, who are of a nervous temperament, find a real temptation in this area of our living. But God is patient, and will help us overcome our infirmities. But we should not and need not yield to the temptation of worry any more than to any other temptation.

If we doubt God's ability to help us, let us ask forgiveness, and cast all our cares and anxieties on Him, knowing He cares for us.

Sing unto the Lord
(Psalm 30:4a)

Cast your care on Jesus today;
Leave your worry and fear.
Burdens are lifted at Calvary;
Jesus is very near.[2]

Verse to Memorize: *Wherefore let them that suffer according to the will of God commit the keeping of their souls to Him in well doing, as unto a faithful Creator* (I Peter 4:19).

A Danger to be Avoided

***For after they have escaped the pollutions of the world through the knowledge of the Lord and Saviour Jesus Christ, they are again entangled therein, and overcome, the latter end is worse with them than the beginning. For it had been better for them not to have known the way of righteousness, than, after they have known it, to turn from the holy commandment delivered unto them. But it is happened unto them according to the true proverb, The dog is turned to his own vomit again; and the sow that was washed to her wallowing in the mire* (II Peter 2:20-22).**

Regardless of how far we have advanced in our spiritual experience, there is a warning here for all. Our adversary is constantly trying to deceive genuine followers of our Lord and Saviour Jesus Christ.

Many true followers of Christ have turned back to their former life of sin. There are those we read of in God's word, such as Demas. In Colossians 4:14, we read, "*Luke, the beloved physician, and Demas, greet you.*" Then in II Timothy 4:10a, Paul writes, "*For Demas hath forsaken me, having loved this present world...*" Something happened in the life of Demas between these two writings of the Apostle. Our enemy is subtle, cunning, and experienced in destroying souls. He would cause one to think he can "enjoy the pleasures of sin" for a while, and then turn about and experience the blessing of God. I had an individual, who was contemplating a course of sin, ask me if God would forgive such a sin. King David said, "*Keep back thy servant also from presumptuous sins; let them not have dominion over me*" (Psalm 19:13a). I wish everybody were as cautious of sinning as this one who asked me if God would forgive such a contemplated sin. I was kind, but very firm in warning of the danger of such a presumptuous sin. Fortunately, this individual took heed and turned away from the sin.

But there is real danger when one tampers with sin. There is an illustration given of a young lady who saw a heavily charged wire hanging from a light pole. She said, "I believe I will just touch it and see if I can get a slight shock." But when she touched the wire, her hand was suddenly gripped by the current and she could not let go.

There she stood, held by the flow of electricity in the wire and crying, "Help me. I am burning up, and I can't turn loose." Her mother came to her rescue and tried to pull her loose, but the current threw her to the ground. A man came along and was able to cut the wire and freed the girl, but not until she was almost burned to death.[1] Sin always takes its captives further than they plan on going.

There is forgiveness for those who genuinely repent, and turn from sin, but it is a dangerous course to follow when one "plays" with sin.

Sing unto the Lord
(Psalm 30:4a)

If you are tired of the load of your sin,
Let Jesus come into your heart.
If you desire a new life to begin,
Let Jesus come into your heart.[2]

Verse to Memorize: *Be not deceived; God is not mocked: for whatsoever a man soweth, that shall he also reap* (Galatians 6:7).

The Only Remedy for Sin

Background Scripture: I John 1:1-10; 2:1-6

***If we say that we have no sin, we deceive ourselves, and the truth is not in us. If we confess our sins, He is faithful and just to forgive us our sins, and to cleanse us from all unrighteousness. If we say that we have not sinned, we make Him a liar, and His word is not in us* (I John 1:8-10).**

God's word does not contradict itself. Cults have come into existence when doctrine is built around some isolated portion of scripture without considering all God's word has to say on the given subject. When we study the entire Bible, then truth falls into focus. So we must study all God says about sin.

There is much controversy when it comes to the doctrine of sin. We as holiness people are often misunderstood when we teach and preach that a man can be delivered and set free from the bondage of sin. Condensing the doctrine of holiness, it simply means to love God with all the heart, soul, body, mind and strength, and to love our neighbor as ourselves. To live above sin, means we live free from all willful transgressions of the known laws of God. From pure motives, we blunder and make mistakes, for which we are sorry, and need the blood to cover, thus praying, "*And forgive us our debts, as we forgive our debtors*" (Matthew 6:12).

But God has made provision in the atonement to deliver us from willful, presumptuous sinning. Anything less is not Biblical. "*Whosoever is born of God doth not commit sin*" (I John 3:9a). "*He that committeth sin is of the devil; for the devil sinneth from the beginning. For this purpose the Son of God was manifested, that He might destroy the works of the devil*" (I John 3:8). This verse does not contradict I John 1:8 that reads, "*If we say we have no sin, we deceive ourselves, and the truth is not in us.*" This latter verse refers to the sinner, before coming to Christ, who deceives himself by saying he has no sins to repent of, when the Bible says, "*For all have sinned, and come short of the glory of God...*" (Romans 3:23)

Years ago, a young lady told me she had never sinned, but she overlooked the fact she was neglecting the house of God, which in itself constitutes a sin of omission.

All committed sins stem from an impure heart. We need to take care of the cause, so that the effect will cease, and to do that, we need first to repent of all committed sins, then surrendering all to God with an unconditional surrender, pray for the baptism of the Holy Spirit, which purifies the heart by faith (See Acts 15:9).

From the time our first parents fell until the present moment, man places blame on others and tries to excuse himself from his own personal sins. I have a precious little great-grandson, who after killing ants said, "These shoes kill ants." Likewise all of us in one way or another have made excuses for ourselves until the heart is changed. My little great-grandson, and all children need to be lovingly but firmly taught the basic doctrines of the Bible in a way that they can understand. They must be lead to Christ before sin takes its toll.

There is a cure for sin. Although God's word teaches us that we are to live free from sin, provision has been made according to I John 2:1-2 for us to be restored through Christ our Advocate if we should be so unfortunate as to sin.

If you have never experienced Jesus Christ as Lord and Saviour, or if you have fallen away or need the further work of the Baptism of the Holy Spirit, why not come to the Saviour now? He waits with outstretched arms to receive you.

Sing unto the Lord
(Psalm 30:4a)

Just as I am without one plea
But that thy blood was shed for me,
And that Thou biddst me to come to Thee,
O Lamb of God, I come! I Come![1]

Verse to Memorize: *A new heart also will I give you, and a new spirit will I put within you: and I will take away the stony heart out of your flesh, and I will give you an heart of flesh* (Ezekiel 36:26).

Love Perfected

Background Scripture: II John

***And now I beseech thee, lady, not as though I wrote a new commandment unto thee, but that which we had from the beginning, that we love one another. And this is love, that we walk after His commandments. This is the commandment, That, as ye have heard from the beginning, ye should walk in it* (II John 5-6).**

God inspired the Apostle John to write this brief book of Holy Scripture. At this writing, Saint John was now advanced in years and supposed to have been about ninety years of age. During his long life, no doubt he had experienced the persuasive power of love, remembering that Jesus condensed the whole law into love for God, and love for our neighbor. Also, our Saviour made love the badge of discipleship when He said, "*By this shall all men know that ye are my* disciples, *if ye have love one to another*" (John 13:35).

When love is lacking, the result is strife, contentions, and division. Satan attempts to divide the Christian Church. It was so at Corinth. We read, "*For ye are yet carnal: for whereas there is among you envying, and strife, and divisions, are ye not carnal, and walk as men?*" (I Corinthians 3:3) These people at Corinth had not as yet experienced the perfection of love.

In this spiritual warfare in which we are engaged, it is hard to fight against the powers of Satan and his forces, while attempting to fight a civil war among ourselves. We do this when we fight against those who preach Christ, but do not conform eye to eye with all our convictions.

Years ago a naval battle took place during a time when Britain and France were engaged in war. This battle was hard fought through the night. As morning dawned you can imagine the surprise of both crews when they realized both ships were British. Each thought they had been fighting against a French vessel. The sailors wept as they brought their ships close, and saluted one another.

I wonder when time shall be no more, and the dark night of the sorrows we experience in this world have passed away, when we greet one another in heaven; will we see how we could have united better as Christians in love to promote our common cause of preaching Christ and Him crucified.

St. Paul was opposed as he preached and ministered. In Philippians 1:15-18 we read "*Some indeed preach Christ even of envy and strife; and some also of good will: The one preach Christ of contention, not sincerely, supposing to add affliction to my bonds: But the other of love knowing that I am set for the defense of the gospel. What then? notwithstanding, every way whether in pretence, or in truth, Christ is preached: and I therein do rejoice, yea, and will rejoice.*"

Of whatever persuasion we are, may all those who love God, unite in loving one another, and promote God's Kingdom on earth, thus, bringing salvation to men, and glory to God.

Sing unto the Lord
(Psalm 30:4a)

Love divine, all loves excelling,
Joy of heaven, to earth come down.
Fix in us thy humble dwelling;
All Thy faithful mercies crown.
Jesus, Thou art all compassion;
Pure unbounded love Thou art,
Visit us with Thy salvation;
Enter every trembling heart.[1]

Verse to Memorize: *Be ye kindly affectioned one to another with brotherly love; in honour preferring one another* (Romans 12:10).

Prosperity and Health

***Beloved, I wish above all things that thou mayest prosper and be in health, even as thy soul prospereth* (III John 2).**

This scripture and many others reveal the fact that God is interested in the whole man. God only asks that we give Him the rightful place He deserves in our hearts and our lives. Jesus said, "*But seek ye first the Kingdom of God, and His righteousness; and all these things shall be added unto you*" (Matthew 6:33).

Because some may have over emphasized the temporal blessings God has promised is no reason why we should avoid or neglect to claim the promise God has made available to His children.

Gaius was a good man and much needed in the life of the church. It would have been impossible for John to have prayed such a prayer, or wish for health and prosperity for a man who was self-seeking, and had his heart set on mammon and things pertaining to this world. But Gaius was a man who could be trusted, and would be a good steward of his health and any material blessings of this life granted to him by God.

As Christians, we should do what is within our power to have a healthy body. We cannot pray for health while neglecting those habits, which aid in producing a healthy body.

While yet a young man I was awakened to the fact that I must take care of my body if I were to live. A serious illness that could have caused my death made it mandatory that I practice the laws of health if I were to recover and continue to fulfill my ministry. Proper food, exercise, rest, and plenty of fresh air, no doubt, helped contribute to my long life.

Our body is the temple of the Holy Ghost (I Corinthians 6:19) and as such, we should not only avoid using the members of our body in what we usually think of as sin but should also do what we can to keep our bodies healthy and fit instruments that God can use.

In our church, divine healing is listed as one of our articles of faith.

It reads, "We believe in the Bible doctrine of divine healing and urge our people to seek to offer the prayer of faith for the healing of the sick. (Providential means and agencies when deemed necessary should not be refused.) We also believe God heals through the means of medical science."[1]

Those who are not healed in answer to the prayer of faith should not despair. St. Paul, when shipwrecked on the island of Malta, was enabled to pray the prayer of faith for the barbarous people, and it appears that all who came to Paul were healed. Yet Paul prayed for his own healing three times and was not healed, but God gave him the promise, "*...my grace is sufficient for thee: for my strength is made perfect in weakness*" (II Corinthians 12:9 part).

Instruction is given in James 5:14-16 as how to pray for the sick. Many good people serve God with frail bodies and should not feel that their sickness is a result of sin in their lives. However, disobedience can be the cause of sickness in some. In that case, the sick should follow the instruction given in James 5:15-16a, "*Confess your faults one to another, and pray one for another, that ye may be healed.*" While on earth in bodily form, Jesus healed the sick. The Scripture says, "*Jesus Christ the same yesterday, and today, and forever*" (Hebrews 13:8). Our God is able!

Sing unto the Lord (Psalm 30:4a)

There's not a friend like the lowly Jesus.
No, not one! no, not one!
None else could heal all our soul's diseases.
No, not one! no, not one![2]

Verse to Memorize: *But He was wounded for our transgressions. He was bruised for our iniquities: the chastisement of our peace was upon Him; and with His stripes we are healed* (Isaiah 53:5).

The Danger of Apostasy

Background Scripture: Jude

***But ye, beloved, building up yourselves on your most holy faith, praying in the Holy Ghost, Keep yourselves in the love of God, looking for the mercy of our Lord Jesus Christ unto eternal life* (Jude 21).**

It is a sobering thought as we contemplate the fact that all orders of beings were created pure and holy, but many, by their choices, have turned to their own ways and apostatized from the "*faith which was once delivered to the saints*" (Jude 3b). Even Satan, one of the archangels, turned from his exalted position and rebelled against God. His influence caused one third of the angels to turn against God. In revelations 12:7-8 we read, "*And there was war in heaven: Michael and his angels fought against the dragon, and the dragon fought and his angels, and prevailed not; neither was their place found any more in heaven.*"

In writing of the awful state of angels and men who were deceived and apostatized from the faith; Jude concludes his message in writing "*to them that are sanctified by God the Father, and preserved in Jesus Christ, and called*" (Jude 1b), warning them of the dangers that led to apostasy, and exhorting them concerning the measures they should take in order to build their faith, thus avoiding this awful state of perdition.

Jude says, "*Keep yourselves in the love of God...*" (Jude 21a). There is a sense in which none of us are able to keep ourselves, for we read, "*Wherefore let them that suffer according to the will of God commit the keeping of their souls to Him in well doing, as unto a faithful Creator*" (I Peter 4-19). Even so, we as God's people have a part we must do in the building and the preservation of our faith. "*But ye, beloved, building up yourselves on your most holy faith, praying in the Holy Ghost, Keep yourselves in the love of God...*" (Jude 20-21a). The truth is we must cooperate with God in order to be kept from the power of Satan and live victoriously.

How do we build our faith? Jude mentions our prayer life. He says, "*praying in the Holy Ghost*" (Jude 20b). St. Paul exhorts the Galatians to "*Walk in the Spirit, and ye will not fulfil the lust of the flesh*" (Galatians 5:16b). We dare not contend in battle with Satan in our own strength for in that case defeat is inevitable.

Also, various Scriptures place emphasis on hiding the Word of God in our hearts. In the wilderness temptation, Jesus resorted to the Scriptures in each temptation He faced. The Psalmist declared, "*Thy word have I hid in my heart, that I might not sin against Thee*" (Psalm 119:11). St. Peter writes, "*As newborn babes, desire the sincere milk of the word, that ye may grow thereby*" (I Peter 2:2). The Apostle Paul tells us to "*Put on the whole armour of God, that ye may be able to stand against the wiles of the devil*" (Ephesians 6:11). There are many other things we are exhorted to do as found in God's Word. Then after having done all we should remember Paul's words to the Ephesians, "*And having done all, to stand. Stand therefore...*" (Ephesians 6:13b-14a)

We are passing through enemy territory and there are many traps and mines set by the enemy therefore, let us be on guard. We read in Proverbs 3:5, "*Trust in the Lord with all thine heart, and lean not unto thine own understanding.*"

Sing unto the Lord
(Psalm 30:4a)

May Thy rich grace impart
Strength to my fainting heart,
My zeal inspire.
As Thou hast died for me,
Oh, may my love to Thee
Pure, warm, and changeless be,
A living fire![1]

Verse to Memorize: *Take heed, brethern, lest there be in any of you an evil heart of unbelief, in departing from the living God* (Hebrews 3:12).

THE CHOICE IS YOURS

Background Scripture: Revelation 22:10-21

***And the Spirit and the bride say, Come. And let him that heareth say, Come. And let him that is athirst come. And whosoever will, let him take the water of life freely* (Revelation 22:17).**

There were those in the time of Ezekiel who said, "*...The Lord hath forsaken the earth, and the Lord seeth not*" (Ezekiel 9:9b). But how blinded these people were in their sin and darkness, "*For the eyes of the Lord run to and fro throughout the whole earth, to shew Himself strong in the behalf of them whose heart is perfect toward Him*" (II Chronicles 16:9a).

God takes delight in revealing Himself to mankind, whether it be Moses on the backside of the desert receiving the Law, or John on the isle of Patmos, writing Revelations, or anyone who thirsts for the Living God.

If God had not taken the initiative, and made Himself known to man, we would be in total darkness without hope. He has always been "*the true Light, which lighteth every man that cometh into the world*" (St. John 1:9b) but not until "*the fulness of the time was come*" (Galatians 4:4) and Jesus Christ tabernacled in the flesh, would we be able to get a clear picture of God the Father. Jesus said, "*...he that hath seen me hath seen the Father...*" (John 14:9).

In Genesis, the first book of the Bible, God revealed to us what has already taken place, but in Revelation, the last Book of God's Word, we have a picture of what is yet to come.

It is not necessary to fully comprehend all the images, symbols, etc. in this prophecy, in order to receive the message God has given us. But there is enough on the surface to stir our hearts to be prepared for that which is yet to come.

Of the many truths revealed in Revelation, God has revealed to us in these last chapters a view of hell that we might be warned of "*...the great day of His wrath...*" (Revelation 6:12) and be prepared, and a view of heaven that we may be encouraged to "*...run with patience the race that is set before us*" (Hebrews 12:1b).

God's word points out clearly that there is coming a day of retribution.

In this world, we see injustice in our courts at times, but "*In the day when God shall judge the secrets of men by Jesus Christ*" (Romans 2:16a), there will be an impartial judgment.

I very seldom have a vision, but God showed me the forces of evil arrayed against Him and His followers until I got a clear picture of the hideousness of sin and the love of God in His wrath and justice dealing with sin. I clearly saw the necessity of a pure heart, and it was an indescribable feeling to be with God and those whose hearts were pure.

Jesus gave many warnings concerning hell. Our Saviour speaks of hell as a place where "*there shall be weeping and gnashing of teeth*" (Matthew 24:51b). There will be no friendship in hell. It is difficult to imagine what I now relate, but Satan had a lady so blinded that she would not accept Christ as Saviour because her husband died without making any profession, and she said she wanted to go to hell in order to see her husband. It breaks my heart to see many people with such blighted ideas.

God's word gives us a beautiful picture of heaven for the blood washed saints in Revelation 21-22. It is indescribable. The best imagery we know here on earth is used to describe heaven, yet it falls short in picturing what God has prepared for those who love Him.

The time is short, but the clarion call still rings out in the last chapter of the Bible, "*And whosoever will, let him take of the water of life freely*" (Revelation 22:17b). But the choice remains for you and me to make. There is danger and death in procrastinating, so why not come to Christ today?

Sing unto the Lord
(Psalm 30:4a)

There's a great day coming, A great day coming;
There's a great day coming by and by,
When the saints and the sinners shall be parted right and left.
Are you ready for that day to come?[1]

Verse to Memorize: *Behold, I come quickly: blessed is he that keepeth the sayings of the prophecy of this book* (Revelation 22:7).

ENDNOTES

Genesis

1. *Worship in Song* (Kansas City, MO: Lillenas Publishing Co., 1972), 341

Exodus

1. *Pointed Illustrations,* 71
2. *Worship in Song* (Kansas City, MO: Lillenas Publishing Co., 1972), 130

Leviticus

1. Ibid., 124

Numbers

1. Ibid., 260

Deuteronomy

1. Ibid., 222

Joshua

1. G. Franklin Allee, *Evangelistic Illustrations* (Chicago: Moody Press, 1961), 64
   This illustration taken from the book, *Crusade in Europe* by Dwight D. Eisenhower
2. *Worship in Song* (Kansas City, MO: Lillenas Publishing Co., 1972), 320

Judges

1. Ibid., 64

Ruth

1. *Sing to the Lord* (Kansas City, MO: Lillenas Publishing Co., 1993), 526

I Samuel

1. *Worship in Song* (Kansas City, MO: Lillenas Publishing Co., 1972), 190

II Samuel

1. Ibid., 129

I Kings

1. Ibid., 284

II Kings

1. Ibid., 70

I Chronicles

1. Ibid., 241

II Chronicles

1. Ibid., 297

Ezra

1. Ibid., 82

Nehemiah

1. Ibid., 339

Esther

1. Ibid., 146

Job

1. W. M. Tidwell, *Pointed Illustrations* (Unknown), 69
2. *Worship in Song,* (Kansas City, MO: Lillenas Publishing Co. 1972), 451

Psalms

1. W. M. Tidwell, *Effective Illustrations* (Kansas City, MO: Beacon Hill Press, 1943) 64
2. *Worship in Song,* (Kansas City, MO: Lillenas Publishing Co. 1972), 1

Proverbs

1. Ibid., 206

Ecclesiastes

1. Ibid., 395

Song of Solomon

1. Ibid., 33

Isaiah

1. Quote from Samuel Logan Brengle of the Salvation Army
2. *Praise and Worship,* (Kansas City, MO: Lillenas Publishing Co.), 409

Jeremiah

1. *Worship in Song,* (Kansas City, MO: Lillenas Publishing Co. 1972), 123

Lamentations

1. Ibid., 349

Ezekiel

1. Ibid., 47

Daniel

1. Ibid., 436

Hosea

1. Ibid., 106

Joel

1. Ibid., 409

Amos

1. Ibid., 90

Obadiah

1. Paraphrased from Oscar F. Reed, Armor D. Peisker, H. Ray Dunning, William M. Greathouse, *Beacon Bible Commentary*, Volume 5 (Kansas City, MO: Beacon Hill Press, 1966), 152
2. *Worship in Song,* (Kansas City, MO: Lillenas Publishing Co. 1972), 197

Jonah

1. Ibid. 230

Micah

1. Albert F. Harper,General Editor, *The Wesley Study Bible* NKJV (Nashville: Thomas Nelson Publishers, 1990)
2. *Worship in Song,* (Kansas City, MO: Lillenas Publishing Co. 1972), 444

Nahum

1. Ibid., 4

Habakkuk

1. Ibid., 450

Zephaniah

1. Ibid., 399

Haggai

1. W.M. Tidwell, *Effective Illustrations* (Kansas City, Mo: Beacon Hill Press, 1943) 115
2. *Worship in Song,* (Kansas City, MO: Lillenas Publishing Co., 1972), 233

Zechariah

1. Ibid., 62

Malachi

1. Ibid., 377

Matthew

1. Abridged by Ralph Earle, *Adam Clarke's Commentary on the Bible,* (Iowa Falls, IA: World Bible Publishers, Inc), 782 Copyright 1967 by Beacon Hill Press of Kansas City, Originally published under the title *Adam Clarke's Commentary on the Bible* abridged by Ralph Earle by Baker Books, a division of Baker Book House Company, Grand Rapids, MI
2. *Worship in Song,* (Kansas City, MO: Lillenas Publishing Co. 1972), 92

Mark

1. Ibid., 281

Luke

1. Ibid., 172

John

1. Ibid., 220

Acts

1. Leewin B. Williams, *Holiness Illustrations,* (Kansas City, MO: Beacon Hill Press, 1940) 65
2. *Worship in Song,* (Kansas City, MO: Lillenas Publishing Co. 1972), 271 (Copyright 1912, renewal 1940 by F. M. Funk. Assigned to Hope Publishing Co.)

Romans

1. W.M. Tidwell, *Effective Illustrations,* (Kansas City, MO: Beacon Hill Press, 1943), 19
2. *Worship in Song,* (Kansas City, MO: Lillenas Publishing Co. 1972), 432

I Corinthians

1. Ralph Earle, *Adam Clarke's Commentary Abridged by Ralph Earle,* (Copyright by Beacon Hill Press of Kansas City, 1967), 1099
2. *Worship in Song,* (Kansas City, MO: Lillenas Publishing Co. 1972), 291

II Corinthians

1. Ibid., 301

Galatians

1. Ibid., 47
2. Ibid., 62

Ephesians

1. Ralph Earle, *Adam Clarke's Commentary Abridged by Ralph Earle,* (Copyright by Beacon Hill Press of Kansas City, 1967), 1186
2. *Praise and Worship,* (Kansas City, MO: Lillenas Publishing Co), 363

Philippians

1. Ralph Earle, *Adam Clarke's Commentary Abridged by Ralph Earle,* (Copyright by Beacon Hill Press of Kansas City, 1967), 1190
2. *Worship in Song,* (Kansas City, MO: Lillenas Publishing Co. 1972), 377
3. Ibid., 333

Colossians

1. Ibid., 44

I Thessalonians

1. *Praise and Worship,* (Kansas City, MO: Lillenas Publishing Co.), 409

II Thessalonians

1. *Worship in Song,* (Kansas City, MO: Lillenas Publishing Co. 1972), 278

I Timothy

1. Ralph Earle, *Adam Clarke's Commentary Abridged by Ralph Earle,* (Copyright by Beacon Hill Press of Kansas City, 1967), 1228
2. *Worship in Song,* (Kansas City, MO: Lillenas Publishing Co, 1972), 377

II Timothy

1. Ralph Earle, *Adam Clarke's Commentary Abridged by Ralph Earle,* (Copyright by Beacon Hill Press of Kansas City, 1967), 1231
2. *Worship in Song,* (Kansas City, MO: Lillenas Publishing Co. 1972), 122

Titus

1. *Praise and Worship,* (Kansas City, MO: Lillenas Publishing Co.), 388

Philemon

1. *Worship in Song,* (Kansas City, MO: Lillenas Publishing Co.), 414

Hebrews

1. Dr. J.B. Chapman, *Holiness Triumphant,* (No copyright)

2. *Worship in Song,* (Kansas City, MO: Lillenas Publishing Co.1972), 290

James

1. Ibid., 467

I Peter

1. Ralph Earle, *Adam Clarke's Commentary Abridged by Ralph Earle,* (Copyright by Beacon Hill Press of Kansas City, 1967), 1195
2. *Worship in Song,* (Kansas City, MO: Lillenas Publishing Co. 1972), 214

II Peter

1. W.M. Tidwell, *Pointed Illustrations,* (Unknown), 117
2. *Worship in Song,* (Kansas City, MO., Lillenas Publishing Co. 1972), 229

I John

1. Ibid., 232

II John

1. Ibid., 16

III John

1. *Manual/1997-2001 Church of the Nazarene,* (Nazarene Publishing House, Kansas City, MO. 1997), 33
2. *Worship in Song,* (Kansas City, MO: Lillenas Publishing Co. 1972), 464

Jude

1. Ibid., 54

Revelation

1. Ibid., 186

www.ingramcontent.com/pod-product-compliance
Lightning Source LLC
Chambersburg PA
CBHW060300050426
42448CB00009B/1703
* 9 7 8 0 8 8 0 1 9 4 7 1 6 *